The colours of sand

...... Jane Austen but hopefully an interesting read, never-the-less. Much love, Subitha.

Tales from an expat compound in Riyadh, Saudi Arabia

Subitha Baghirathan

◆ Tangent Books

www.tangentbooks.co.uk

Unit 5.16 Paintworks
Arnos Vale
Bristol
BS4 3EH

richard@tangentbooks.co.uk

0117 972 0645

First published 2012 by Tangent Books

ISBN: 978-1-906477-83-7

Design: Bertel Martin, Joe Burt (joe@wildsparkdesign.com)

Printed in the UK using paper from a sustainable source

To David:
who makes everything seem possible

For Riya and Shivani:
you are my greatest adventure

Acknowledgements

I must thank Bertel Martin from City Chameleon for all his efforts along the journey, since early 2011, to get this book from my computer screen out into the world. I also thank Richard Jones from Tangent Books for his help during the last stages of this project. I am proud to have worked with two local, independent publishers. The final message of thanks goes to my parents. The list of my reasons would be too long.

Content

Biography

Subitha Baghirathan is a Sri Lankan who has lived in UK for most of her life. Through her father's career, Subitha spent many years of her early childhood as an expat in Indonesia. As a teenager, she frequently visited Bangladesh where her parents were working at that time. As part of her degree at the University of Edinburgh, she studied in Germany and Russia. After a year gaining work experience in Bangladesh, Subitha completed a Masters in Social Policy at the University of Nottingham. All her work – life to date has been in the voluntary and community sector.

She and her partner, David, have known each other since they were children. David's family also spent time outside UK as expats when he was growing up. For the past ten years, Bristol has been their home, with their two daughters. In March 2009, the family relocated to Riyadh, Kingdom of Saudi Arabia, where they lived on an expat compound. This book is an account of those times from Subitha's perspective.

Disclaimer: the names and some of the circumstances of people in this book – exempting family members – have been changed to protect their identity and privacy. All the anecdotes are either based on Subitha's direct experiences or those shared with her by other expats. There is no intended offense towards the country, its religion and culture or to any of her fellow expats.

Introduction

Bristol, October 2007: my partner landed a promotion; a three year overseas posting in Riyadh, Kingdom of Saudi Arabia. Out of our family of four, I was the only one who hesitated at this offer. I saw myself diminished under the black shroud of an abeya, against a backdrop of monotonous, yellow sand, the call to prayer providing a repetitive soundtrack. Yet, simultaneously, I was enticed by the lure of shedding wellies and cagoules, to relocate from a country where autumn seemed eternal, to a place promising 20 degree warmth even in its winter months; and an outdoor life for my young daughters. Beyond all that was the prospect of a family adventure to a country that remains so little known to so many.

A decision was made: the contract was signed. In March 2009, the female trio of our family joined my partner in Riyadh, where our home for the next two and a half years was a Western, expat compound. This is my story of those years. The challenges were harder and different to my expectations but many of my experiences affirmed my life rather than diminished it. It proved to be a time far more varied than the yellow sand first promised.

The Beginning

It was only later that I felt grateful for the fact that my arrival in Saudi Arabia was made under the cover of darkness. Not because the night sky coaxed me into irreverence, encouraging me to undo my tightly buttoned-up abeya and thrust the black headscarf I had been clasping anxiously back into my bag. *That* casual confidence towards my Saudi "uniform" came only after about half a year of my life had been spent in Riyadh.

No, the gratitude was to the cover the darkness gave to Riyadh that first evening, rather than to me. My first excursion into the unflinching daylight and reality came the next day and it exposed a landscape totally alien to me. I needed that first night's sleep to deal with it. "Lunar" is how a cousin describes it; he had spent part of his childhood in Riyadh in the 1970s. The capital city of the Kingdom of Saudi Arabia had changed significantly since then: three-lane highways stretched in every direction; glass-fronted shopping malls and tower blocks, seemingly fashioned out of enormous cubes of ice, vied with each other for splendour and height; and sprawling, walled compounds – to accommodate non-Saudis – were scattered here and there, the tops of their well-tended date palms just visible over the barbed wire and machine gun turrets.

But these were just pretenders to the throne; the desert was king. The recent, oil-funded concrete landscape did not keep back the existence of the desert – always so near, pervasive and insistent. And lest you forgot its power, the desert reminded you by suddenly letting forth a sandstorm that made the SUVs on the highways stumble into each other; that shrouded Riyadh's tallest building in an hour; that crept through your air conditioning system; and filled your mouth, eyes and ears if you were foolhardy enough to step out into it. Some expats maliciously said that when the oil runs out and the expat workers leave en masse, all the new infrastructure developments will simply be reclaimed by the desert.

In Riyadh, a mere 15-minute drive out of the central business and high-end shopping districts took you to areas where vast swathes of the desert surrounded you. That 15-minute drive also navigated through areas that looked derelict – unfinished buildings stared reproachfully at passers-by, looking like the stuff from one those documentaries on 'Holiday Hotels from Hell'. On Day Two in Riyadh, my oldest daughter asked why so much of Saudi was a building site. Here was one of my first discoveries of the many conflicting aspects of Saudi Arabia. We moved to Riyadh as the grim reality of the recession was making itself felt in UK. We relocated to a country that we knew would not need to implement "austerity measures" – wealthy as Croesus due to its natural asset of oil. It was therefore a shock to see parts of Riyadh that looked like a third world, developing country, with tumbling-down dwellings marooned on dusty vacant lots, wild dogs limping around and an old, abandoned car rusting serenely on the sidelines.

During those first excursions off the compound, my brain was in furious protest at what my eyes were taking in. I realised how spoilt my sense of sight had been up to this point. My memory banks hold slide shows of images of Sri Lanka – my homeland. Shady trees laden with fruit such as mangoes, jackfruit, rambutan. Hindu temples fronded by jasmine-flower curtains. The shiny, wet greenery of Nuwara Eliya's tea plantations. I left Sri Lanka at the age of one but continued to visit regularly. Since then, my homes have included Indonesia, Scotland and Bangladesh. My main base, my point of frequent return, is England. My most recent surroundings there – snow piled up on the sides of footpaths and red-bricked semi detached houses – felt as distant from this lunar landscape as the humid green of the tropics. Suddenly, all that colour seemed surreal, even a little obscene, as my eyes and brain tried to adjust to the unrelenting yellow of the desert.

During our time in Riyadh, we occasionally undertook the five-hour drive to Bahrain, almost the whole journey of which is through desert. My partner, David, exhorted me and our daughters to look out of the window to spot all the different colours of the sand. It remains one of the most striking examples for me of his enviable ability to seek silver linings in every cloud. For the girls and me, however, our enthusiasm for this particular car-game was a non-starter: "It's all just yellow, Daddy!" By the time we arrived in Riyadh, David had been there for about eight months on his own. The girls and I had remained at home in UK, trying to out-stare the Saudi visa process. We were eventually granted our visas in an odd coincidence, after I had purchased an English copy of the Quran and David had romantically gifted me my first full-length, jet black, shapeless abeya. God moves in mysterious ways; or "Inshallah", as was frequently said in Riyadh. During that first eight months, and continuing during our time in Riyadh, David had to frequently drive to Taif for work – a seven-hour drive across the desert to the west coast of the country. Small wonder, therefore, that by the time we reunited as a family in Riyadh, David had assimilated so well to his new environment that – like a Bedouin – he now could see different colours of sand in the desert.

There are those who will accuse me of being overly dramatic, perhaps a little spoilt even. My "inside" world of the compound did give me not only the colour green, but also the shocking pink of the bougainvillaea, the blue of the swimming pool and flashes of white on the chests of the miniature gazelle who roamed freely about. By extreme luck, we were the last people my partner's employer housed on our compound, due to the exorbitant rent prices that increased every year. There's no denying that it was one of the nicest compounds in the city, designed by an American woman who was a close friend of the Saudi compound owner – or so the urban myth went. Most compounds tend to be built in that tried-and-tested urban design I have experienced in cities such as New York and St Petersburg: a nice, clear grid with blocks of housing or offices dissected by straight roads. On compounds, this style is very bleak and uninviting: square houses, straight roads and little greenery. Our compound was a true oasis: built not in a grid but a butterfly shape.

Untold expense kept a nine-hole golf course watered, green and lush for residents, golf club members and the miniature wild gazelle. We lived not in houses but "villas", with slanting roofs and balconies. One area of the compound was taken up by a little farm, with chickens, goats, peacocks and a restless white horse. All compounds have pools, but we had a choice. There was a quiet little pool, usually child-free, by the "condos" or apartments. Then there was the main pool, where you could swim lengths in one section, which is what I believe pools are made for; dive from a platform in another, deeper area, which is all David ever wants from pool time; or go down the long, windy slide in yet another area, which is what our daughters wanted to do all day long, every day. On a raised area, there were also two little shallow pools for babies and toddlers – although, to be honest, with the nature of their outdoor compound life, it was rare to see a child from the age of three who wasn't a strong and fearless swimmer already.

Physically, it was like a holiday complex. A colleague of David's visiting from UK exclaimed: "It's like Centre Parcs!" I came to realise that living in Centre Parcs longer than two weeks, in a country like Saudi, was not as rose-tinted as the spectacles would have you believe. The majority of professional Western expats in Saudi are men. Thus, Western expat women in Saudi tend to be "accompanying spouses", either with or without the accompanying baggage of children. Most compounds in Riyadh have a kind of United Nations roll call for the nationalities of their residents: from USA and UK, Swedes, South Africans, Australians, Canadians, Indians. I could go on. Given the culture and restrictions on women in Saudi, many expat women, myself included, found it difficult to get suitable employment in Saudi – a subject I will return to. Therefore, once all the men had driven, or been driven by their drivers, in their SUVs off to work in the mornings, the compound was dominated almost totally by the presence of women. I would sum it up thus: we were a group of women, diverse in our nationalities, backgrounds, beliefs and hobbies – contained by the compound walls, with a forced, shrunken day-to-day existence, where we mainly only had the opportunity to mix with other women like ourselves, generally doing the same things as each other, day in, day out.

I was activated into feminism at the age of 16 by an aunt in Sri Lanka and definitely don't denigrate being in all-women company. However, I did not find this situation a powerful opportunity to share experiences with or learn from other women – as I have in the past when in all-female company. Moreover, whatever the diversity and range we had experienced in our lives pre-Saudi – as professional working women, or in the interests we had – once we got to Saudi, this all became narrowed down to a life where the main activities included the weekly food shop, coffee mornings, dominoes or golf lessons. This was even more excruciating for me as a feminist, as I went from a domestic situation in the UK where my partner and I had earned roughly the same amount and shared the mortgage, the cooking and holiday childcare – to one where I did all the cooking, laundry and childcare while my mortgage contributions and financial clout dropped to zero. The same was the case for the majority of other women on the compound. I became one of a line of women queuing at the compound dry cleaners to pick up my partner's work shirts, rushing back to make dahl for dinner before picking the children up from school. Because our compound rents were so high, companies often put their more senior employees on it – for whom they could justify the expense. So, many of the "accompanying spouses" had been doing just that for decades, following their husbands' careers around the world. While I was in my not-so-honeymoon period of this lifestyle, this had been their way of life for a much longer time. I'm sure they probably couldn't see what all my fuss was about. Living on a compound in Riyadh long-term just wasn't for me in countless ways. Accepting David's new-found belief in the different colours of desert sand was the easiest thing to adjust to.

There were some women who kept a very low profile on the compound and appeared to not want to socialise at all, a tendency I increasingly had more empathy with. Like in small communities everywhere, it was quite easy to find that details of your family, career or unspent criminal convictions were known by people you hadn't even met yet. I had an overwhelming urge to stuff my fingers in my ears on a few occasions when a resident divulged intimate medical details of her neighbour to me. Nevertheless, I found it a little eerie at times, to be out and about and go past a villa that I knew housed one of the compound's reclusive Marlene Dietrich characters. I wondered if she was sitting lonely and miserable inside, hoping someone would remember that the villa was in fact inhabited – or if maybe she was relieved to not have to endure another tedious conversation about how bad the ovens were in the villas' kitchens. I mused about what she did all day, with her husband at work, and no children about. Most of the mothers on the compound had no choice of totally opting out of socialising, with their children clamouring to hang out by the pool as soon as homework was done, or wanting to have a play-date over. There was one woman resident, who appeared to wait until it was dark, when the avenues emptied of playing children, before scurrying out to buy a much-needed pint of milk from our little shop. I would infrequently pass her in the dusk, when I was out on a training run or en route to teach yoga; my cheery greeting usually met with a word-less, quick smile. I used to joke to David that there were probably times when she would send her driver to the nearest supermarket to get the milk, rather than walking to the shop herself, for fear of perhaps bumping into another resident and feeling obliged to make small talk.

Teasing aside, I did feel sympathy for those who really struggled with how – or how not – to be sociable on the compound. The life can be very superficial: at times it was reminiscent of Freshers' Week at university, when everyone was trying too hard to make friends – by making a lot of effort to seem the wittiest, the trendiest or the most alternative student in the year. People often told their "back story" in a zippy, presentation-style eight minutes, after which point you were assumed to know them well and were officially "FFL" – friends for life. Making friends as an expat, particularly on a compound, can feel like that at times.

The other side of the coin is that people can leave at the drop of a hat, with job contracts terminated with the twist of a prayer bead. Even without the sudden, surprise departures that characterised Riyadh expat life, the very nature of that type of world includes the constant goings of old friends and comings of new people who might become friends. David and I were able to take this in our stride as we had spent much of our earlier life as expats with our parents. David believes that this history is partly why he is never overly interested in making or having many friends. Apart from not being able to live without me, obviously, he is the most self-sufficient person I know. One of my favourite poets, John Donne, wrote that, "No man is an island, entire of itself", but David would have liked the chance to challenge him over that statement. However, some people really struggled with this "symptom" of expat life. After making and then having to say goodbye to too many close friends, one woman simply brought down the shutters and chose to live an almost solitary life, simply unable to put herself through the emotional upheaval of expat friendships any longer.

I moved to Riyadh in March 2009 with my two daughters, Shivani and Riya – joining my partner, David, who had been based there since July 2008. Ostensibly, we went to Saudi through a job opportunity for David. In reality, we had harboured plans to spend some time overseas, outside UK, while we were a family with young children, even before the children themselves were actually a reality. I dimly remember those halcyon days with just the two of us, able to make a Saturday disappear by spending all day on our bikes in the countryside, revved up by the fresh air and talking non-stop; and the times when we happily looked up from an intense conversation to find ourselves in a past-last-orders pub "lock-in". Those are the days squarely to blame for me ending up in Saudi Arabia because it was then that we discovered shared ambition to go abroad while we had young children, inspired by our own vibrant, happy memories of our childhoods as expats in Indonesia. We both agreed that our best experiences abroad with our families had been before the age of

10 – and that we wanted the children we eventually would have to also have this. David and I had both subsequently spent time abroad as adults, on our own initiative. In the early days of our relationship, we were often on the verge of going off abroad again together. We decided instead to postpone it temporarily: to settle down a little; think "career" rather than simply "job"; buy a house and have our children – before letting the wanderlust seep back in…

I'd spent almost a year working and living in Bangladesh before David and I got together. I had made it clear that I would go anywhere but a strict Muslim country again. When David mentioned a job vacancy in Saudi Arabia advertised at work, my initial reaction was that he had got the infamous "seven year itch". I thought this was his way of letting me know he wanted to go off on his own again. But no – he wanted us to go as a family. This was the opportunity he had been pestering his employer for since he joined them, a few months into our relationship. Not many other employees wanted to go to a country like Saudi, but there was young David Nicholls, who'd been like a bee in a bonnet about an overseas post since Day One. He even said his family were keen to join him. This is something employers are usually warm to, as this means you are more settled in the country and job, and less likely to want to leave suddenly. It was a "no-brainer", as the saying goes. David was offered the post.

We then spent three months deliberating about taking it up. We had been partners for eight years at this point. Without question, it was the hardest period of our relationship – even harder than becoming parents for the first time. When our first daughter, Shivani, was born, we were equally enraptured and petrified; but she was physically there and we just had to get on with it. Discussing whether we'd made the right decision or not to have a child was rather a moot point by then. During those three months, however, the element of choice was so stressful, with the added responsibility of making a decision that would change the lives of four people. Like a mosquito bite you can't help but itch, it was all we could talk about when we were together. It took over our conversation and every spare space in our heads. Although many of our anxieties were by no means resolved when we finally made the decision to go, a huge burden lifted for me. The choice had been made; and I have a reputation for stubbornness. I promptly set an embargo on talking about Saudi for at least a month in an attempt to salvage David and my relationship.

When the girls and I finally got to Riyadh, the process had taken almost 18 months from that date. I looked out of the SUV window into a star-less sky, wearing my abeya as a statutory necessity for the first time ever, and breathed in the hot desert air. I wondered whether this was the right moment to try to remember the many, many lists of pros and cons we had filled every available bit of paper with, back in autumn 2007. I decided, for a change, to savour the moment.

"Marhaba": welcome to the beginning; the beginning of some of the tales of my time in Riyadh, Kingdom of Saudi Arabia.

Things to see and do

A large-hearted, highly efficient British woman – formerly a resident on our compound – set up an information system of "stuff going on", distributed via email to anyone who signed up with her. This system was taken up by another "pillar of the community" after its founder returned to UK. Through this email system, I would get dates of illicit piano recitals at embassies; flyers for the latest production by the Riyadh expat am-dram society; "For Sale" lists from the lucky departees of Riyadh and so on. In the Wahabi interpretation of Islam, cultural activities such as music, art or drama are forbidden. All artistic expression should be channelled into religious worship. In my former life, I used to revel in monthly visits to an art house cinema; a rainy Saturday afternoon could entail taking my daughters to wander around an art gallery; and once a month, I would timidly venture out to a writing group for Black and Asian women, where I would hide my poems but listen admiringly to the writings of other members.

An expat like me could feed my cultural habit by grasping at the occasional straw of a concert by one of Riyadh's two choirs and once by a sculpture exhibition bravely and clandestinely hosted in the basement of a Saudi woman's house. The concerts and plays took place at embassies or compounds. The former, in particular, gave protection from a potential raid by the muttawa (religious police). Embassies are hallowed ground, in their own way. Some of them are situated in the "last season's" palaces of members of Saudi royalty, which further strengthens the feeling that you are a little more out of the reach of the muttawa than usual. Moreover, the opulent fixtures and decoration of the palaces added to the "other-worldliness" of the evening's experience. The delicious pleasure of live music would be further sweetened by the complimentary canapés and glasses of non-home-brewed red and white served in the interval. This "carrot" was what persuaded David to join me at one of these concerts – classical and choral music usually provokes an allergic reaction in him. As a true engineer, he immediately became quite absorbed in the maths behind the singing – how the voices knew when to come in and out of the music and what notes to sing; and how the conductor managed to guide them through the pieces. Our friend in the choir showed him some of the sheet music they had just used and David was struck dumb at the complexity of it all. It took an extended stay in a country where live music is forbidden to make David a more open-minded concert- goer.

The Saudi working week runs from Saturday to Wednesday; our weekend is Thursday and Friday, the latter being the Islamic holy day. One blistering hot Thursday morning, my family went along to an art exhibition advertised via the usual expat email channel. I didn't have high hopes; I wasn't expecting some roomy art gallery with a trendy coffee shop; I just wanted desperately to get beyond the compound walls and do something as a family, out of the sun, that didn't involve shopping malls. In Riyadh, apart from the main highways which are generally named for members of the Saudi royal family, most roads have neither name nor number. Thus, to find private homes, other compounds, embassies etc., people fashion maps on the computer, showing you how to find them, using the nearest large, named road as a starting point. This is what you were given instead of someone's address. The only reason this was consistently successfully for us is due to David's never-failing sense of direction and memory for roads and landmarks. His job prior to Rolls Royce involved him driving hundreds of kilometres on his own, across unmapped CIS[1] farmlands, in the days before mobile phones and Satnav. Trying to get to an isolated farm somewhere in the depths of Uzbekistan before nightfall, or end up spending a frozen night in your jeep, is a pretty good incentive to become adept at finding your destination. For some couples and families, trying to locate someone's home using these homemade maps could bring a relationship to the brink of divorce,

---

1   Commonwealth of Independent States: the countries that formerly made up the USSR.

from some of the tales I heard.

This particular Thursday morning, David drove us into an obviously wealthy residential area. Expansive villas were hidden behind tall, long stretches of walls. The average Saudi home is usually either built behind walls as tall as Rapunzel's tower or with tiny, high-up, prison-like windows – or both. This is equally to protect the fairy tale princesses inside from the eyes of unfamiliar men; and to save the men from the tempting sight of the women within. When we arrived, I was the one to get out of the car and announce ourselves on the intercom. If David had done this – an unknown, white man – he could well have besmirched the reputation of the women of the home, as well as exposing all of us to the risk of a muttawa raid. It need only take one phone call from a nosy, malicious neighbour to set this in motion. The hostess of the art exhibition was already raising her head above the parapet by her actions. I'd had to pre-book a time for our visit, so she knew exactly who to expect and when – for security purposes.

Once we'd navigated all these potentially explosive social tripwires, it was a golden morning as we met the artist and viewed her sculptures, which were housed in an underground bunker-type room, with skylights scattered in the roof to make it a perfect, light space for exhibiting art. I was burning with questions for the artist – a rare opportunity to speak with a Saudi woman on her own territory. I wanted to ask about her views on her homeland and its customs. How could I not be curious about her life as a working artist in a country where she could not exhibit publically or even let it be known she created art, for her safety's sake? However, I didn't want to offend her dignity or seem like a bigoted expat, searching for sensational stories of oppression and ignorance in Saudi Arabia. The artist showed neither of these qualities as she talked with us about the concepts behind her work, relaxed and confident in her skinny jeans and gamine haircut. She showed us her kiln and workshop, also housed in this villa complex – the home of a good friend. This was the person who promoted and made all the arrangements for the exhibition, whom we subsequently met as we were ushered into a large conservatory, lined with elegant, cushioned sofas, perfectly accessorised with a table of bounty: a silver jug of Arabic coffee, little dishes of dates, miniature cakes and pastries, and fruit overflowing a silver platter. Our hostess was a working woman in her own right – in addition to supporting her friend's artistic work. She ran a travel agency, specialising in tours to Saudi historical sites, which were open to expat families and also single expat women. These tours were thoughtfully scheduled over weekends, making them more accessible for the expat clientele.

Travelling around Saudi as a single woman – whether expat or local – is extremely difficult, particularly if it's in the pursuit of tourism rather than business. At least if you are a business woman travelling around, you have the sponsorship of your employer to lend legitimacy and purpose to your solo travel. Through ingenuity, determination and a heavyweight contacts' list, this Saudi female travel agent was able to allow single expat women on her tours: they stayed in hotels, in a room on their own, alongside the families also on the tour. They all travelled together on planes out of Riyadh, then on coaches to their destination. These mixed groups would also eat together, usually in a large private dining-room at the hotels they stayed at. Thus, unaccompanied women – either single or married – intermingled with married men travelling with their families. It really is complicated to convey to people who have never been to Saudi what a feat this travel agent achieved in making these tours happen.

Saudi women have to have permission to travel within and without the country from the significant male in her life: father, husband or uncle. This also extends to non-Saudi women who hold other nationality passports but are married to Saudi men. An assertive, intelligent teacher from Australia I once worked with left me speechless when she told me she had to have a letter from her husband to present at the airport, to enable her to go and visit her family in Australia. She had an Australian passport, so a visa to enter her home country was not the problem. Rather, the issue was being allowed to leave Saudi without her husband. This white, Western woman had converted to Islam on her own account whilst still living in Australia, and then subsequently met and married her Saudi husband when she came to Riyadh to work as a teacher. Both she and her husband saw no place for this rule in their Islamic faith. However, the fact that they were in an unorthodox, mixed-race marriage probably gives away their more liberal attitudes, compared to the average Saudi family, who may not question such regulations.

The ability to travel within Saudi is made more difficult by the fact that many hotels will not allow single female guests to have a room. A female colleague of David's based in UK had to stay in one of the corporate suites on our compound when she came to Riyadh for work. Visiting male colleagues from UK, on the other hand, were always put up at one of the five-star hotels in town.

I often got "cabin fever" from my family while we were in Saudi. David worked away from home frequently; during the worst period, he worked in a different location away from Riyadh every week for over a month, commuting back to us at weekends. This aspect of his job had definitely not been spelled out to us when the post was offered to him. Single-parenting on our compound was an aspect of my Saudi life I struggled with far more than my infrequent interactions with the muttawa, who had represented my biggest anxiety before I got to Riyadh. When David was with us at the weekends, he was always very supportive, encouraging me to go off on my own, away from the children and him. But the choices were scant: go to a shopping mall or go to a shopping mall. Once there, you could either browse, bust up your husband's salary or sit in the food court and comfort eat.

During my years in Riyadh, I never saw a Saudi woman sitting with a book, magazine or newspaper out in public – be it at the doctor's surgery, in a mall café, or airport lounge. The only reading matter I occasionally saw a Saudi man with was the Quran. This may be the only text that people are encouraged to read under Islam. I wager that fiction set outside the Middle East would be frowned upon as portraying ways of life too contrary to Islam. Such literature may offer a reader some escapism from the quotidian customs of Wahabism. For someone who spends a not negligible amount of my time immersed in the shelves of a library, it was a shock that there appeared to be no public libraries in Riyadh. There was one chain of bookshops – with at least two branches I frequented – which surprised me by selling quite a range of books. For adults and children alike, there was a decent range of fiction and non-fiction, in both Arabic and English. I was perplexed to find an English language translation of a book by a Saudi woman that had been banned in her home country. There didn't appear to be the original Arabic version of the book for sale. Undoubtedly, Saudi people must read; the books available could not have been intended purely for the expat market. However, I speculated that reading in public might be seen as un-Islamic; you could be seen as indulging in entertainment and diversionary activities. As an aside, Arabic is written the other way round from English – from right to left – so Arabic books open to the right. My younger daughter, Riya, used to occasionally read the right-hand page of her English language books first, telling me that she thought it was an Arabic book, when I pointed out her mistake.

Sometimes it is only the absence of a routine, detail or characteristic that makes you realise it was ever there. This desert of public reading brought home to me how awash UK is with people immersed in a book or newspaper – at bus stops, on the tube, on benches at children's playgrounds, blissfully oblivious to the calls of their children to "Watch me, Mummy!" I take a book everywhere I go, even to the supermarket, where a long queue at the till may offer a couple of minutes' reading time. Yet again, my general behaviour set me at odds with Riyadh society. I would look up from my book – at the doctor's surgery or whilst my daughters played in a mall play area – to find myself the object of puzzled scrutiny by the Saudi mothers or Filipino nannies sitting on nearby benches. Thus, David's kindness, urging me to take my book to a local café or mall, did not evoke the enthusiasm in me he had hoped for. My preferred option was to turf him and the girls out of the villa – for quality pool time together – while I got on with some more studying in peace.

In my former life, I used to be able to get away occasionally: to attend a conference for work, or to spend a weekend with my brother in London. Those options were not available to me in Saudi. I therefore resolved that I would go on one of these tours on my own, during the next winter season. Regrettably, my resolution was never carried out, as the winter weekends of 2010/11 quickly filled up with our running and cycle club events. The winter months were prime time for Riyadh's sporting calendar. Before I knew it, it was April and already too hot for any more tours. This unticked item on my Riyadh "to do" list gave yet another pressing reason to return there, for another expat period in the future, from David's standpoint, at least.

The Aviation Museum

One happy discovery for family outings was the Aviation Museum. Thanks to that ever-industrious email network, we went along on a tour organised by a small ex-pat community group. The event was led by an energetic, welcoming Western woman who openly described herself as a "happy housewife". I kept turning this phrase over in my head, playing with it like a ball, wondering whether I could ever see myself using that label without lacing it with sarcasm. The moment certainly hasn't happened yet.

The museum was an oasis, a world away from vacuous shopping malls and walled compounds. A clean, spacious building, enclosed by vast glass windows. Inside, old helicopters and small aeroplanes casually lounged, which we were allowed to clamber into, press all variety of buttons and yank about joysticks. Our daughters loved it. David's second engineering career saw him change from an agricultural engineer, working on combine harvesters and tractors, into an aero engineer. He was in a natural home here. We were so pleased with ourselves for having the place in our clutches.

To explain this feeling, some background is needed. There are very few museums in Riyadh, so finding this one, a mere 20 minutes' drive from our compound, was wonderful. The hot summer months start from May and last until October. David and I always had our antenna up for indoor things to do at weekends during the hot season, to give us and the children a different and more rounded experience than simply more pool time.

Places like museums and the zoo have an added complication. They run on a strict timetable. Firstly, as a given, everything in Riyadh shuts for the five daily prayer times. Added to that: most places shut all afternoon from 1 until 4pm and virtually nothing is open on a Friday. Secondly, opening times in museums and the like are demarked for different groups of people. There are "men only" times; family times; and "women and children only" times. At Riyadh zoo, the timetable affects the animals, too. The male elephant is not allowed out of his housing during "women and children only" times: supposedly, women should not see his rather large and obvious genitals without being supported by their father or husband. When I visited Riyadh zoo on my own with my vulnerable daughters, I personally was delighted not to have to go through this ordeal without David's manly support.

The Aviation Museum had a sensible family slot – Thursday mornings – which meant not only could we go on a family outing there, but I could also take the girls on my own whenever I was stuck for something to do at a weekend when David was working away. Usually, by Thursday morning, the compound walls threatened to rob me of my last dregs of sanity and goodwill. I always wanted to get off the compound and do something with the children at this point in the week.

One fine Thursday morning, I had an interesting experience at the Aviation Museum. We had been dropped there in a compound taxi and found we had the museum totally to ourselves. The girls proceeded to fly me gallantly to a number of different destinations in helicopters and other small aircraft. I had a thermos of coffee and a book; we were ready to settle in until midday, when our taxi had been booked to collect us. Then a large party of Saudi men arrived,

whom I labelled as a "fathers and sons" outing – there were lots
of teenage boys and older men. Unfortunately, the teenage boys
could not believe their luck at being able to ogle at and lurk near an
unaccompanied woman, shrouded in a black abeya, but with her hair
and face uncovered. My bhindi, mukuthi (nose-stud), large earrings
and loose hair suddenly seemed like lots of little red flags to a pen
full of young bulls. I felt horribly self-conscious but, as always out in
Saudi, tried to hide this from Riya and Shivani. I worked hard to try
to minimise all the negative views of femininity and the female form
that were all around us, ripe for them to pick up on. I was determined
that the three of us would not leave Riyadh uncomfortable in our
gender.

The "fathers" of the group were as mortified as I was but for
different reasons. They did not expect to encounter someone like me
there – an unfettered non-Islamic woman, with two mini versions
gaily frolicking at my side. They went for a pre-emptive strike. I
casually suggested to my daughters a wander around the first floor
of the museum, where there were various flying suits to look at, with
the ulterior motive of getting away from the men. While we were
up there, a security guard was dispatched to bring an abrupt halt
to our visit. He brusquely reported that the museum was shutting
immediately – half an hour earlier than scheduled. No reason was
given but it was glaringly obvious to me that the "fathers" had
demanded that the thorn in the side of their weekend activity was
removed. I was now faced with the situation of standing outside in
the blasting 40-degree heat, in the museum car park, with my young
daughters – no shade, benches or air-conditioned coffee shop in sight
– and a 30-minute wait for our taxi still ahead. Frankly, it served me
right for adorning myself with such big earrings and jaunty bhindi,
but I did feel guilty that Shivani and Riya had to pay the price for my
vanity that day. Luckily for us, our kindly taxi driver had arrived early.
As we sped out of the car park, I saw the local branch of "Fathers for
Justice" get off their minibus and troop back into the museum, smug
in the knowledge that it was now an exclusive all-male environment,

as, indeed, the entire world would ideally be.

The Shebab

Our family wasn't alone in searching for things to do in Riyadh. Groups of "shebab" seemed to have an equally frustrating time. This term is used to denote a non-traditional teenage Saudi boy. He is most commonly distinguished by his expensive designer slouchy jeans, strategically frayed T-shirt, funky hairstyle and gaggle of friends, all similarly dressed in this louche style. Untold amounts of Saudi oil dollars must be spent to look so scruffy. In other words, the young men who reject wearing the ankle-length, white thobe, sober haircut and beard of the traditional Saudi man. These young men were regularly denied entry to shopping malls and restaurants merely on the strength of how they look. Breaking from conformity is not encouraged or tolerated in Saudi – it is a perceived threat to the status quo and an affront to the religious way of life.

The shebab have wealth that allows them expensive designer wear and a smorgasbord of "toys": mobile phones, quad bikes, high-performance cars. What their money cannot buy them is the must-haves of teenage life for most Western teenagers: girlfriends or even just friends of the opposite sex, going to the cinema, watching their favourite band live in a concert, trying to sneak into a pub under-age. A reflective friend described their situation as akin to that of some super-rich celebrities – rich thanks to mummy or daddy's wealth, awash in cash but searching for some real substance and direction in their lives. The shebab do not need to have a work ethic or be driven by an ambition for a particular career; regardless of their academic achievements, most middle-class Saudi young men are assured of a more than decent, permanent job in the private or public sectors once they finish their education.

Their frustration and boredom emanates from them as strongly as their designer aftershave. On a Wednesday night on Olaya Street, the Riyadh equivalent of LA's Rodeo Drive, I once watched groups of shebab, unprotected by helmets or suitable clothing, on quad-bikes, racing each other, going up the road, in the opposite direction to the flow of traffic. On a misty Friday morning in January, in a taxi, heading out of the city to a running race at Dirab golf course, I was confronted by a gathering of high-performance sports cars, the revving of their engines loudly audible over the sound of music in my ears from my iPod. I questioned the taxi driver about this; he said that groups of shebab often met in this area to race each other as the sun went up. Just as David's cycle club met outside the city for their fortnightly races, to escape the censorship of the muttawa, so too did these young Saudi men. It seemed that they needed to get a little of their pent-up energy out of their system, before the day's first call to prayer, when they would be expected to join their families to mark the main Islamic day of worship. Images of "Saudi surfing" are also available on YouTube: a shebab will surf on his expensive shoes along the road, holding unto the door of a high-performance car or SUV, driven at breakneck speed by a friend.

In 2007, a World Health Organisation report on road traffic accidents and young people found that this was one of the leading causes of death for 18-24 year old young men in the Middle East and Africa.[2] I harbour hopes that the shebab who manage not to die before the age of 30 may become the catalyst for future change in Saudi Arabia. As they grow older and take up their positions in "the establishment" – such as jobs in banks or the civil service – they will be much better placed to gently help along a relaxing of certain regulations and attitudes, perhaps more so than Saudi women en masse or the well-intentioned international community.

Small pebbles can still build a bridge, it is said. This next generation of husbands may not insist their wives wear black gloves and sunglasses – in addition to the abeya and hijab – when outside the home. They could choose to not take up their right to have a second wife if the first does not produce sons. They could encourage their daughters to study professional qualifications, whilst asking

---

2   World Health Organisation 'Youth and Road Safety' 2007.

their sons to take a turn cooking a family meal occasionally. In their work life, they may be able to discreetly encourage applications from female candidates and ensure skilled women are not confined to dead-end jobs. I am a dreamer, who will not stop hoping that a growing number of these Saudi young men will slowly and subtly effect some change in their country in these and other personal actions.

Under cover of darkness

Whilst David and I were constantly on the look-out for daytime weekend activities for the family, Saudis, it would appear, slept or hung out in their homes. As the sun set and we were getting our children ready for bed, Riyadh's shopping malls, camel souks, go-karting tracks and all other array of leisure activities burst into life, thronged by Saudis. Whereas it's like water in the desert to find something interesting to do with children at 10am at the weekend, at 10pm, these choices are like oil in the Saudi desert. All these places opened from 4pm until at least midnight, and often to 2am at the weekend. On the rare occasion that David and I would venture off the compound for dinner on a Wednesday night (equivalent to a UK Friday night), on our return journey home to relieve the babysitter at 11pm, we'd drive past children's play arcades, malls and modern-style souks, lit up like lighthouses and bustling with people.

My peevishness aside, this lifestyle is totally understandable given the climate, plus the frequent breaks in the day for salat (prayer). The last prayer time is usually between 6-7pm. Following this isha'a prayer, there is a wide window of opportunity – up to around 3am the next morning – for shopping, family activities, picking up your freshly dry-cleaned thobes, ordering more bling from the Gold Souk and so on. As a family, we were totally inept at adapting to this timetable. The school day starts and ends early in Riyadh – again, in a bid to manage the afternoon heat. My alarm clock was always set for 5.45am, a source of frequent complaint from me – I am not a morning person. Thankfully, from the day she was born, Riya has been, so she was usually cheerfully awake before my alarm clock had even rung. Shivani's preference is more akin to mine: she had to be shoe-horned out of bed at 6.15am, to get ready for the 7.15 arrival of the school bus. These early hours became set in all our body clocks, whether it was the weekend or school holidays. Thus, a lie-in during a Riyadh weekend constituted sleeping in until 6.30am at the latest. This proved extremely rare thanks to our dawn-worshipper, Riya. David and I added icing to the early bird's worm by crazily choosing hobbies with events usually starting around 7am on Fridays. Thus, on alternate Fridays, either he or I would excitedly creep out of the house at six in the morning to take part in our cycling or running races. At times, this choice seemed questionable even to us. We did show a little sense, though, by not competing in some of the triathlon club events that entailed a 4.30am race registration time.

There were a few Saudi and other Middle Eastern children at Riya's Montessori school. One day she brought home a birthday party invite from a school friend soon to turn three. This particular pool party was due to *start* at 8pm on a school night, a time by which both my children would have already been in bed for an hour and only an hour earlier than my own bedtime. I turned down the invitation, much to Riya's annoyance. In our usual topsy-turvy way, for our daughters' joint birthday party in June, to beat the heat, we arranged a breakfast party by the compound pool starting at 8.30am. By 10.30am the party was over and everyone went indoors, taking refuge in the air conditioning.

Camping under a flyover
Whilst we resisted cultural conditioning into the Saudi daily schedule, we *did* appreciate their love of camping and al fresco eating. These customs are part of the traditional Bedouin way of life. It felt good to see that the oil dollars didn't homogenise everything in its path. Camping shops in Riyadh offer an extensive and expert range of kit: less fast-food outlet and more organic, home-grown, fair trade produce for the discerning camping palate. As well as tents, there are wonderful, thick, canvas-backed rugs, resplendent in the colours of

Joseph's dream-coat; little triangle-shaped stools, for propping your arm over whilst you recline and nibble on dates; and old-fashioned hurricane lamps for when the sun sets. This equipment would be used for picnics as well as full-blown camping. From rather humble beginnings, we quickly acquired some proper kit for the picnics we frequently had during the cool season; not least to save face. There was a wadi area in Riyadh that was turned into a park and picnic area, complete with little footpaths and compact, bricked-off earthen squares for traditional wood-fired barbequeing. We used to go there regularly on a Friday morning for breakfast picnics. We started off by taking little rag rugs to sit on, a thermos of tea, bottles of water and juice, pots of fruit and jam-filled croissants. This was suitable at the time of the morning when we usually were there, as there were rarely any Saudis there at that time on a Friday. However, by late morning, Saudi families would begin arriving, following prayer time, and promptly put our picnic to shame. Out of the SUVs, came thick rugs, bolsters, little stools. Once all the women and children were settled comfortably, one of the men got a fire going in the little barbeque patch, whilst the meat was brought out: chunks of lamb, chicken legs, fat beef sausages. A kettle would also be settled unto the hot fire to make fresh pots of Arabic coffee in the shiny silver coffee pots that had been brought along. Proper pottery bowls of fruit were arranged around the rugs, alongside jaunty little bowls of dips like hummus, labneh, motabal, to be dipped into with the Arabic bread piled up by them – large, round, soft and droolingly fresh. As you can tell, our family watched all of this very closely, taking care not to lick our lips too loudly. I also surreptitiously tried to hide our Tupperware sandwich boxes and thermos, in an attempt to pretend we were simply down at the wadi for a walk and play at the playground. Picnicking? Us? No – not as you know it, anyway.

The wadi was a picturesque place to picnic, a perfectly rational site to set up temporary camp for a weekend open-air lunch feast. However, some Saudis seem to be content to picnic in much less salubrious spots, making choices that seemed quite peculiar to me. Under highway flyovers; in the middle of hectic main road intersections; on a narrow strip of dusty ground, sandwiched between a building site and yet another main highway. I liked to imagine that the Saudi families who did this were very traditional; more attached to their Bedouin roots than to the Westernised, oil-fuelled lifestyle of their peers. Perhaps these had been places their families had always picnicked in when they were children, and they were adamant they would continue this tradition, regardless of whether these particular spots now formed part of the modern landscape of highways, flyovers and shopping mall car parks. If this really was the case, I would have to admit to a grudging admiration for them rather than worrying that the lunatics had escaped the asylum.

Segregation

I have already talked about the timetable dividing the opening hours of places of interest into distinct slots according to gender and family status. There was also physical segregation in certain places to contend with. Eating out is a large part of modern Saudi life and the range of eateries is vast. Alongside the usual suspects of fast food pizza, burgers and fries outlets are very expensive, high-quality restaurants offering cuisine from around the world: Japanese sushi; Indian restaurants with authentic tandoor ovens; haute cuisine from France; Turkish restaurants where sesame-dotted flatbread the length of the table is brought out. When I completed my law course, a close friend – a female Spanish lawyer who had got over all the hurdles to secure a relevant job in Riyadh – took me to celebrate at a Japanese restaurant where diners sat around special tempanyake tables and watched their fish, steak and baby corn sautéed in front of them.

This meal out was a rare occurrence for me. Try as he might, David found it hard to get me off the compound to try out the different restaurants in the city. My aversion was based on a number of irrefutable nuisances: the traffic was consistently awful; we couldn't enjoy a nice glass of wine with our meal; I had to keep my abeya on; and we had to sit in a separate family section of the restaurant. The last point on my list of "Reasons not to eat out in Riyadh" deserves some explanation. Restaurants and cafés had two separate areas, including two separate entrances. Usually, the area that looked most appealing to eat in would be the men's section, entered via a "men-only" door. This section would be airy, open plan, with lovely décor, sometimes including an outdoor dining area. The family section loomed behind the "family section" door. I remember watching a live performance of the Black comedienne, Angie le Mar, who complained about what happened whenever she took an idea for a programme to a TV producer. She would be told to take her idea to the "Multicultural department", a department which spelled doom to her. My feelings about restaurants' family sections echo Ms le Mar's sentiments. These sections typically consisted of lines of booths, partitioned off by a black curtain or screen. Not only families but also groups of unchaperoned women were able to dine in these sections. Being totally curtained off from other diners meant a woman could unbutton her abeya if she wished or perhaps even take it off. I personally seldom did this because I then had to watch out for prying eyes, whenever the waiter opened the curtain of the booth to take our order, or serve our food. The paranoia that Saudi's regulations provoked in me made me certain that it would be mere minutes before an outraged male Saudi diner would catch a glimpse of me in a near-nude, non-abeya clad state and chose to alert the muttawa of immoral behaviour going on in the restaurant, resulting in a raid by them. David just rolled his eyes when I cited this reason for keeping my favourite item of clothing on during a meal out.

The muttawa are the Saudi Arabian religious police, with a role and responsibilities separate from the regular state police. Their headquarters was the Ministry of Vice and Virtue, situated next door to the fondly nicknamed "Chop chop" square, where judicial sentences such as the chopping-off of hands were carried out in public on Fridays, the holy day. The muttawa's uniform consists of long white thobes, the optional beard down to the chest, maybe accessorised with some prayer beads. Some muttawa chose to wear their thobes at calf-level as a sign of their piety, referring to a significant episode in the Quran. The muttawa were a range of ages, not just the wizened old men I had stereotypically envisaged before I moved to Riyadh. There was salacious gossip in expat circles that the muttawa visited jails, encouraging certain prisoners to repent and embrace a more strictly observed Islamic life. An option was then given to be educated appropriately to join the muttawa, rumour has it. The muttawa can be found roaming inside malls and souks, popping their heads into restaurants and idling in cars in mall carparks. Regarding their latter haunt, my view is that they wait in cars, ready to leap out and admonish the woman without her headscarf on, whilst she is struggling with a laden trolley with the ubiquitous single dysfunctional wheel. IKEA was allegedly a favourite raiding place of theirs as the store was not always punctual when closing its tills for prayer times. They can turn up at restaurants, too. Their responsibilities here include making Saudi men leave their dinner to attend a mosque, if their inspection occurs during a prayer time; checking that all women are suitably attired in abeyas with heads covered; and ensuring the decorum of mixed dining groups. This latter inspection entails checking that women diners are there chaperoned by a male family member – father, husband, brother or uncle. There are expat couples I know, particularly those in mixed-race relationships like David and me, who always ensured they took along a copy of their marriage certificate when going out for a meal. As it is, all expats are advised to carry their iqama photo ID card with them whenever leaving the compound. I can't say exactly what the procedure would be in a situation of a woman being out and not suitably chaperoned – with a mixed group of colleagues, for example – as I never experienced it. From anecdotes, I gleaned that the outcome would depend on the attitude of the particular muttawa involved. The dining party could be broken up and sent home. Or the offending mixed group might have to listen to an impromptu lecture about morality whilst their food went cold and rising stress levels killed off their appetites. Those would be the least frightening and preferable options to being taken away for further questioning, which could happen too.

The muttawa did not have a universal right to go anywhere in Riyadh. Western, expat compounds and the international hotels in the city centre were a few of the places denied to them. A high-end mall, oozing with very expensive designer brands had recently been built; it was owned by a well-connected Saudi prince, I was told. He had secured an agreement that the muttawa could not enter this mall. By no coincidence, one of the few restaurants I was happy to go to was securely tucked away there. It was the family section, not the men-only section, that formed the main part of this South-East Asian restaurant – an open-plan area with long wooden tables and benches. So not only could groups of diners see each other, but different groups sometimes had to share a long table. Despite the murky social waters we were swimming in, I thought everyone coped admirably with this. Despite the mall being so obviously for those dripping in wealth, the restaurant was priced for us mere mortals. It was very relaxed and informal, down to the tear-off, pre-printed menus on the tables, on which you ticked your order to give to the waiter. One of the reasons I liked this restaurant was that it appeared to be a favourite spot for birthday meals for teenage Saudi girls. It was unusual and so lovely to see a large, loudly exuberant party of young Saudi women out together, able to relax in the knowledge the muttawa would not appear during their festivities. One evening I was there, the giggling birthday girl went from table to table round the restaurant, sharing out slices of her gigantic chocolate birthday cake, approaching mixed-gender tables of unknown diners, a potentially risky step in many other places.

Some of the restaurants in the international hotels permitted abeyas to be removed. The tempanyake restaurant I was taken to also boasted a central, open-plan family section, with the men-only section a poky little affair alongside. As this was in an international hotel, abeyas could be removed. I was presented with one of the many incongruous sights of Riyadh I will always remember. A white

Western expat woman sat at a table in the ubiquitous little black dress the fashion magazines are always telling women they should own, blithely eating and chatting in a large mixed group of diners. At the neighbouring table, a traditional Saudi couple were seated, not attired in anything featured in a Western fashion magazine. The man wore a white thobe and the woman a black abeya and niqab (full head and face veiling). To eat whilst wearing the niqab appears to be a dextrous feat. The woman had to lift the veil that was draped over her nose and mouth ever so slightly, taking utmost care not to actually reveal any of the lower part of her face. Her other hand then delicately conveyed forkfuls of food up under the veil into her mouth. Sensibly, I thought, she ignored the chopsticks that were also available on the table. As I slurped up a bit of miso soup from its bowl and wiped my chin, I marvelled at her skill.

On a passing note, sights like this will always be reminiscent of Bahrain for me. It was very common to see around the pool of an international hotel, a silent table of Saudi Muslim women totally covered up in abeyas, niqabs, sunglasses and even sometimes black gloves, in the 40 degree heat. They would look on as their husbands or more often nannies played in the pool with their children. Sitting next door to them would be a raucous table of young Middle Eastern women – perhaps from Lebanon, Syria or Bahrain itself – in miniscule bikinis, sharing a sheesha pipe, choosing to remain impervious to the ogling of the nearby Saudi men. Human beings really make a fascinating, infinite study and I feel lucky to have had a stint of social anthropology study in the Middle East.

The subject of segregation in Riyadh is not complete without a mention of Kingdom Tower. This is another high-end mall and also a famous landmark in the city, due to its Sky Bridge. For a modest price, you can take the lift up to the 33rd floor and walk along a bridge, enclosed by glass. The city is all around you – under your feet and stretching out to your left and right. It was a definite "must-see" place for the rare visits of family members over our years there. The second floor of Kingdom Tower is for women only. I was told, not long after arriving in Riyadh, that this was a place I should try to go to whenever compound life specifically and Saudi life in general was overwhelming me. I assumed that being a women-only floor meant I could hang up my abeya once I stepped off the escalator. A male security guard acts as a sentry at the bottom of this escalator, ensuring no men get a chance to dash up there. The café on this floor was staffed by Filipino women – a situation worth mentioning because every other kind of service outlet in Riyadh was staffed by men, mainly from the Philippines or from the Indian subcontinent. To really convey the picture: every single café or restaurant waiter, every supermarket cashier and every assistant in the whole gamut of shops across Riyadh was male, including in lingerie and cosmetics shops. Thus, the café waitresses were a special dispensation reserved for Kingdom Tower's sacrosanct second floor. However, female shop assistants were obviously far beyond the realms of decency, so this role was still carried out by men in the second-floor shops.

My disappointment once on this hallowed ground was huge. Abeyas remained on. After excitely taxi-ing away from the female-dominated quotidian world of the compound, I simply entered another world perpetuating gender segregation. I'm a proud feminist, but that provides me with no sense of duty to go to a women's only shop floor to buy my clothes. I feel there's no need for me to elaborate on why the second floor of Kingdom Tower never became my "bolt hole" when compound life became too much.

I had been looking forward to buying some clothes without having to waddle around the shops in my black sack. I'm fluid and flexible on a yoga mat; put me in an abeya and I walk like a heavily pregnant woman. As I had to keep my abeya on on Kingdom's second floor, my shopping spree never happened. During my years in Riyadh, the only clothing I bought was sports clothes: to teach yoga in and for running. In other words, the staple clothing items for my job and lifestyle there. I found it almost impossible to buy any "frivolous" non-sporting clothes and the fault lies squarely with the abeya. Clothing shops in Riyadh do not have changing rooms for obvious reasons – no risk can be taken of a male shop assistant potentially seeing a woman wearing less than an abeya behind a changing room curtain. Whenever I did spot something I liked, I would waddle over and find the nearest mirror to hold it up against me to see how it might look. All the mirror threw back at me was the image of an anonymous woman shrouded in black, holding some incongruously pretty, colourful item against her shapeless body. My interest in buying it instantly withered. Invariably, the item got put back on its rail. I kept my wardrobe going through my once-yearly summer holidays back in UK, when I would go on a splurge in charity shops, my clothing outlet of choice.

While there was segregation in places like restaurants and gyms, in other places the genders intermingled: supermarkets, any other kinds of shops, souks, children's play areas, hospitals. Something that consistently tickled me was the food court in one of the malls. Signs on the walls indicated separate family and men-only sections but the entire food court was open plan, so all diners effectively sat and ate together. Other food courts tended to have segregated areas separated off by frosted glass screens or wooden partitions. Certain places went to such absurd lengths to uphold gender segregation that it guaranteed to get a smile from me rather than provoking my frustration. Most malls had children's play areas that you had to buy a swipe card for and credit with money. Cards were purchased from a little kiosk, in which sat just one worker, but it was split into two counters with two tills. You guessed it: one side for women, the other for men. The lunacy of this was two-fold. The entire, undivided counter was so small that men and women had to stand side by side in their separate queues, only to be served by the same cash assistant. Once they had purchased their swipe cards at their gender-designated till, they proceeded into the non-segregated play area.

Childcare

From my experience as a child, following my parents' expat life around Asia, I've heard British expats hanker after a myriad of different things from their home country. Marmite; 'Coronation Street'; supermarkets; and cold, dark Christmases when you can snuggle up inside tinselled homes, eating warm mince pies in front of the TV. In Saudi, many of the yearnings are predictable, considering that the country is based on strict, Wahabi Islam: gin and tonics; bacon sandwiches; the cinema; being able to shop without having to keep a watchful eye on the next closure for prayer time. For women expats, there are particular freedoms that many eagerly anticipate when returning to their homeland: being able to drive; shedding the abeya; being out without a thought of the muttawa popping up and shouting, "*Haram!*[3] Cover your hair in Arabia!"

All these yearnings applied to me too, during my years in Riyadh. However, during my last year there, perhaps the thing that most excited me about my prospective return to UK was the provision of good quality, flexible, safe childcare. It sounds so parochial and domestic, but for me this was the one single item that would give back more of my freedom than being able to drive again.

Part of the problem was my previous work-life. For a happy and memorable period, I had worked in early years education, running an education resource centre that aimed to support diverse and anti-discriminatory practice. Bwerani was home to a range of resources including dual language story books; wheelchairs for our multi-ethnic dolls; hand puppets of female doctors, firefighters and police officers. I also ran training in this area. Through this work, I spent a lot of time with some remarkable women, who had real vision and belief in the importance of good quality childcare, particularly for under fives. I learnt vast amounts that not only enhanced my work, but also spilled

---

3   means "woman" in the Arabic spoken in Saudi Arabia.

over into my family life. When I became a parent, these values shaped how I set about bringing up my children. After my year's maternity leave, I chose a childminder to care and educate my daughters on the days both David and I worked. They didn't start nursery until they were three – as recommended by my former colleagues. Although I cannot speak Tamil fluently (my parents' mother tongue), I made an effort to use some basic vocabulary at home so my family would gain some awareness of their ethnic heritage. In short, I have high standards for the childcare and education of my children – both from me and David, and any other sources too, such as their childminder, nursery or school. I should have hung up these standards with my winter clothes before leaving UK for Saudi, because they became a rod for my own back, as David gently liked to remind me.

The school day in Riyadh begins before 8am and ends around 1pm – to manage the heat. These school hours forced me to turn down the full-time post I was offered at the United Nations a month after arriving in Riyadh. They are also the reason a lot of my memories of my daily life there involve long, hot afternoons with both my children home from school, looking for different things to do with them and make the time pass until their dinner time, when David returned from work. I used to fantasise about the after-school club attached to Shivani's school in Bristol. Memories of the wonderful childminder both my daughters went to part-time from the age of one became misty around the edges. During our last school year in Riyadh, I mentally counted down the days until both my daughters were at the same school, where their school day would not start before the sun was visible and would continue to the decent mid-afternoon time of 3.30pm.

I don't want to be misunderstood – I love my children and have prioritised them since becoming a mother. I took a year's maternity leave for each child; negotiated part-time work; and have deliberately not pushed my career onwards and upwards because of the possible fall-out on my daughters. At the same time, my work away from the children always gave me the energy and enthusiasm for my days with them. I found the amount of time I had to spend on my own with Riya and Shivani on the compound really tough. This was exacerbated by David's frequent work trips out of Riyadh; plus the fact that I'd just spent eight months as a single parent in UK, juggling part-time work, part-time studies and full-time parenthood, whilst waiting for the visas that would enable us to join David in Riyadh. I arrived in March 2009, burnt out from family responsibilities, just in time for David to be sent to UK on work for a week, a mere seven days after our arrival. This set the tenor of the whole of our residency in Saudi.

The childcare available to me was made up of "nannies" or maids, predominantly from the Philippines or Sri Lanka. I use the term "nanny" loosely, because the type of childcare and education provided did not correspond to the stereotype of the traditional English nanny, with her impeccable training, strict discipline and routine, and her important status within the family. The nannies I'm talking about often could be seen pushing babies around the compound in their prams, mobile phone permanently tucked between ear and shoulder. Discipline of their older charges could be rather erratic, as they were not always accorded the status and authority within the family to exert any real control. I heard one charming expat child tell his nanny that he'd get his mother to sack her. The nanny seemed to have confidence in this threat, so gave up her efforts at curbing him destroying a ride at the playground. When I collected Shivani from school, I used to watch horrified, as children lobbed their school bags at their waiting nannies, without a word of greeting or thanks, before hurtling off with their friends.

My former early years colleagues told me that the status of childminding only really rose when formal training and qualifications began to be required for the work. This argument is persuasive and I saw this issue bearing some of the responsibility for the status of some of the nannies in Riyadh. Prospective employers, of course, were keen to obtain references from former families nannies had worked for, but any formal training in childcare and education was not a realistic expectation. Added to this, there were literally hundreds of nannies on the prowl for employment at any given time, so it was really a buyer's market. In my first month on the compound, I received a daily cold call or doorstep enquiry from a nanny asking for work. Hence, a six year old with the personality traits of Stalin could give a nanny goose bumps by threatening her with being sacked.

My parents were brought up in Sri Lanka and "ayahs"[4] were a feature of their home-life, and the home-lives of all their friends and extended family. I was born in Sri Lanka, where a full-time, live-in child-carer was also a feature of the first year of my life, before moving to UK. Thus, the role of a nanny was not new to me when I moved to Riyadh. What I hadn't anticipated was how much time I would find myself spending in the company of nannies. Taking my children to birthday parties, only to find myself the only parent there, amongst a bevy of nannies, always remained shocking to me. Another favourite example of mine is the Fun Bus. This was a vehicle with a string of little carriages behind it, festooned with a red-and-white candy-striped awning, which trundled on a 20-minute journey around the compound on Thursday mornings, playing tinkly children's songs on its merry way. During our first year in Riyadh, I often took the girls on this fun-filled extravaganza – a good excuse to get out of the villa. By Year Two, I refused to go on it with them, telling them I'd put them on it and collect them at the end of the ride. It was not unusual for me to be the only parent on the Fun Bus. On all the other benches jostled little children, minded by their nannies. My favourite Fun Bus moments were when I was surrounded by Filipino nannies, who talked loudly in their mother tongue together, over the tinkly music, while I felt like some kind of freak from a Victorian fair. "Come, behold, the curiosity of a woman who looks after her own children!"

With my Sri Lankan heritage, I should have been comfortable with the idea of employing a full-time nanny for my children. I fully acknowledge how hard most nannies worked, and for pay that

---

4   An Indian subcontinent term used to denote a domestic worker whose principal role in the household is as a child-carer. It's a term that educated, middle-class Sri Lankans supposedly try to avoid now, as it is seen to have rather disparaging connotations.

was rarely equal to their input. Some nannies were wonderful carers and educators, too. These were the women who were ferociously head-hunted by other families, particularly if there was a merest hint that their current employer was imminently going to be relocated. A fellow running club member had succeeded in nabbing a much-sought after nanny, whose childcare expertise, culinary skills and truly lovely character were the stuff of urban myth on numerous compounds around the city. Erin happily paid her nanny over double the usual salary, plus a flight home to Sri Lanka every summer while she returned to UK with her children. As both she and her partner worked full-time, she was determined to hang on to Nini and fend off any advances from other prospective employers.

"Having staff" just wasn't for me. Many of my fellow residents, however, took to it like a duck to water. In a paradox to me, they mainly came from countries where employing this type of domestic worker generally is not done, or cannot afford to be done: countries such as Sweden, USA and France. How did these expat mothers segue much more effortlessly into this set-up than me? Some headed families who had been following a career expat father around the globe for many years already. These were the parents who advertised on our compound, via the email information system, for a full-time nanny before even stepping foot in Riyadh. For other mothers, this was a first-time experience, which seemed bumpier for some than others. I observed one newly-arrived expat mum change nannies every three months or so. The adage of the "grass being greener" can obviously apply to one's staff, too. She put herself and her two young children through emotional stress in her endeavours to adopt the trappings of rich expat life. Another Australian mother must have led this kind of life in a past incarnation as an Indian princess she embraced it so wholeheartedly. Like many of the rich Saudi families, she employed a full-time nanny per child. With a full-time driver, part-time cleaner and an ad hoc helper for the ironing, her house appeared rather uneven in its ratio of staff to family members.

For a minority of expat mothers who did not do any paid work, "having staff" could be seen as an expression of status and wealth, as important to fitting in certain circles as driving around in a golf buggy in designer sportswear and having flawless nail varnish. An acquaintance told me of her experience of going along to a resident's coffee morning on a neighbouring compound, where the sole topic of conversation involved sharing horror stories of "staff" – the nanny, driver and maid. However, there were other factors behind hiring a nanny that I had empathy for. There were a minority of mothers who had the right skills and motivation, topped by a little bit of luck, to get themselves jobs off the compound. For these mothers, this type of childcare was the only option to enable them to do the jobs they loved, continue their careers and preserve their own identity and sanity. For expat mothers with a baby or young child under two, life could become very isolating and monotonous, as there were no playgroups or any other kinds of baby and toddler activities around to break up the day and provide escape from the villa. Having a nanny around to share the load was the only alternative activity. Other mothers were probably as bored and frustrated with those long post-school afternoons with their children as I was. If I had dropped my principles and standards like the hot bricks they were, I could have had afternoons off, working on my golf swing or joining in the Wednesday afternoon three-hour dominoes games, while Shivani and Riya played with other children at the playground, their nanny sitting nearby with all the other nannies, keeping an irregular eye on them. It might have made me a nicer person for David to live with, but I wouldn't have been able to live with myself.

Of course, as I settled into my new home, I met other expat mothers like myself – other Victorian curiosities who chose not to employ a nanny for their children. I worked hard to set up informal arrangements with these mothers: "I'll have Kazue over on Tuesday afternoon to make collages with Riya and Shivani. Could they come to you next week, to try out your new ice-cream maker?"

My own issues about not hiring a nanny centred on the quality of childcare and education I could expect to be provided for my daughters. From what I observed both on and off the compound, I didn't have much confidence that the average nanny would be creative, disciplined and involved with my daughters. Without a doubt, I saw and got to know some lovely nannies who were devoted to their charges, who would get down on the carpet to build Lego towers and were strict about manners. However, I felt my children would know they were being cheated in some way by this kind of care. One episode springs to mind: I was at the compound Children's Library with my daughters one afternoon, about one month after my arrival. Six months later, I ended up taking over the running of this service. Many children were brought to it by their nannies. I was sitting on the floor, reading aloud, Riya and Shivani snuggled in and a pile of books in front of us. I suddenly looked up to find out that the children there with their nannies had all drifted over and settled themselves around us, hungrily listening in to the story. My daughters were immediately territorial, verbally swatting the interlopers away: "*Our* mama is reading *us* a story." English was often at least the third language many nannies spoke, with varying degrees of fluency, after their mother tongue and Arabic. Understandably, being able to read English was not a skill every nanny had, so not a lot of reading to their charges went on during the library hour. I intermittently used to let other children join in when I read, or when I was doing other activities outside the villa with my daughters – and encouraged Riya and Shivani to try to be generous with my time and attention too. However, during my last few months on the compound, I increasingly found my former goodwill and generosity in this vein rather sluggish. I became less inclusive about whom I would allow to join in with activities I was doing with my daughters: behaviour I was not proud of and that was not in keeping with the person I had been before I moved to Riyadh.

Riya and Shivani tended to feel sorry for the children who were generally out in the care of nannies. Moreover, after a couple of dismal experiences, they vetoed further play-dates at our house with children who arrived, nanny in tow. The nanny usually followed the children about as they played, or sat in the corner of the room, furiously texting on her mobile, sporadically glancing up to check on her charge. When the children began anything vaguely boisterous, the nanny intervened to either stop the activity, or try to calm things down. For my daughters and the sons of another non-nanny-hiring friend of mine, the mere threat of leaving them with a nanny was an effective deterrent to bad behaviour.

The quality of my parenting was sometimes questionable, but its quantity was irrefutable. Over our time on the compound, as the girls matured, they showed me in little ways how much they valued all that time they had with me, as opposed to with a family's employee. I heard Riya listing to David all her friends who were dropped off and picked up from school every day by their driver, expressing relief that that was not what happened to her. "Mama and I bike to school together every day!" she triumphantly told David. By the end of our second year, whenever David was away over a weekend, both daughters would declare that they would help me out because they knew by then that I found it hard on my own – giving empathy to a usually impatient, short-tempered mother, which I don't think they would have developed if they had had a nanny in tow for the past two years. A range of people – from other mothers, to fellow residents, to the compound taxi drivers – regularly told me that my daughters were the best-behaved children on the compound. While I struggled to not get too depressed at being a solo parent again, when David was sent away on yet another business trip, their teachers reported how consistently happy and sweet-natured both girls were. I left Riyadh rather emptied out of enthusiasm for childcare. Nevertheless, it seemed clear that Riya and Shivani had benefited from all I had poured into their daily lives. Finally, at the end of it all, my convictions on how I wanted to bring up my children remained unshaken, even if I felt a shadow of my former self.

Other compound workers
There was a bevy of other manual workers who beavered away on

the compound to keep it up to the high standards expected from its affluent Western residents. Whereas our home in the UK had a dicky boiler in the winter and the state of our garden frankly brought the neighbourhood down, our villa and the communal grounds around us in Riyadh were maintained to standards for which we were both appreciative and grateful. As far as I'm concerned, the compound gardeners, taxi drivers, maids and maintenance men worked harder than the white-collar executive residents – under the blistering sun, for longer hours, seven days a week, for pay I deliberately avoided enquiring about, for fear of guilt I would never shake off. On our particular compound, most of these workers were from the Indian subcontinent: Bangladesh, Sri Lanka and India. Once my own Sri Lankan identity was ascertained, a particular protectiveness was shown towards me and my daughters – the only residents with Indian subcontinent heritage on the compound – although there was obvious disappointment that I didn't speak Tamil (my parents' mother tongue) or any other Indian subcontinent language. The fact that the girls and I were consistently friendly and polite to them helped. A maid from the compound, Nina, cleaned our villa one morning a week. Another maid, Flora, babysat in the evenings, whenever David was away on work and I had yoga classes to teach. My daughters and I always greeted Nina and Flora when we saw them on the compound and I brought them small gifts back from our holidays. Nina told me that many of the other residents for whom she cleaned would not deign to acknowledge her in public. Yet again, I chose to be a walking-talking paradox to this by taking the gaggle of gardeners who worked in our cul de sac regular cups of tea and biscuits. There were times when I had just sat down in the villa with my own well-deserved cuppa, when Riya would spot one of "our" gardeners outside and demand that I get up and quickly make him a cup too. On significant dates – such as the girls' birthdays or Eid – I used to ride around the compound on my trike, handing out *"mishti"*, a Bangladeshi custom of giving out sweets on important occasions that I'd learnt from my parents' decade of working in Dhaka.

These gestures were repaid in many ways. During our last year there, David and I began allowing Riya and Shivani to go out on their scooters around the compound together for 20 minutes or so on their own. This was something many of the other compound children were allowed to do from a very young age, and often for the whole day at weekends. I bumped into another mum one Thursday afternoon, who told me it was "fantastic": she hadn't seen her nine year old twin daughters for almost six hours and had no idea exactly where on the compound or in whose villa they might be. This was not David and my style of parenting, but we did want to start giving Shivani in particular more independence. One of the reasons I felt confident at the idea of them going out and about on the compound without us was the distant but watchful eyes of the gardeners and other workers. Whenever one of our daughters had a tumble, someone inevitably swooped in, dusted off the injured girl and saw her home safely. When Riya's scooter was "borrowed" from the front of her school one day, the gardeners became very upset at the disappearance of "Baby's" scooter (Shivani was generally referred to as Daughter Number One; I expect that although they knew full well the girls' names, they thought it might be construed impertinent to use a resident's children's names). I roved the compound on my trike, while the gardeners downed tools to locate the missing scooter. In the end, inevitably, it was one of them who found it.

All the workers from the Indian subcontinent treated me with a respectful warmth. From speaking to me about my family background in Sri Lanka, they worked out that I came from an educated middle-class family. The fact that I had been educated in UK and had degrees from two British universities seemed to confirm my status. On the other hand, an unexpected stress arose for me that appeared to stem from a combination of me not hiring a full-time nanny and my informal behaviour and attire. The problem I encountered was from some Filipino maids, who appeared to think that I came from a similar working- class background to them. I was aware that I did not carry with me the gravitas and accessories of a proper rich, expat wife.

With tongue firmly in cheek, David used to ask me to wear more bling to prove my status. I chose to eschew designer sunglasses and sending my children out with a nanny, in favour of cycling about with them on my trike, generally attired in sports clothing, as I invariably was either planning to go for a run or teaching a yoga class at some point in the day. Moreover, my trike was actually the signature transport for maintenance workers on most other compounds outside ours. David had bought it for me as a carrot to Riyadh after my grief at discovering that I had to leave my treasured bike and little bike-trailer behind in UK. My image did me no favours in certain circles.

What I saw as my principled stand to not hire a nanny was something I had expected other expat mothers to find quizzical. I had not anticipated that some nannies might see this as an indication that I too may formerly have been a nanny and maid. One afternoon's play session in our back garden left me crying on David's shoulder, wailing, "She thinks you married your maid!" I had broken one of my golden rules and invited a friend to send her child over with her nanny, Marina, to join in the afternoon of parachute games I had planned for my daughters and two of their friends. The other children were old enough to be dropped off with me. This particular child was much younger and needed someone in tow. I was running around with the children, giving instructions and helping out, aware that Marina was watching my antics with unconcealed curiosity. When I stopped for a breather, she looked at all the children and asked me brusquely, "Are any of these children actually yours?" She worked at a villa in our cul de sac so must have seen me with my daughters a couple of times a day. Who had she thought I was all this time? I looked at the little children around the parachute – with four different nationalities and physical appearances – and realised that Marina thought I was another nanny with whom the parents had left their children for an afternoon's supervision. The air went out of the parachute just as it went out of me. I never answered her question. And I never invited another child with nanny in tow to my home again.

I was in the privileged position of often being an incredulous observer to what other residents got "their staff" to do. Children would be left with nannies for a week or so whilst their parents went off for "quality time" together, perhaps skiing or to a romantic beach destination. Some residents went to considerable expense and effort to get the family dog brought to Riyadh, only to give their driver the task of the daily "walkies". A particularly hard-working driver might have to fit in this task between buying the family's food supplies from the supermarket, taking "Madame's" worn-down shoes to the local cobbler and making the household moonshine. On one memorable occasion, I dropped off a child's birthday present to her villa, interrupting the nanny and driver beached on the living room floor, surrounded by the apparatus necessary for filling 20 party bags. The birthday girl was having a pre-party nap upstairs; her mother was having her hair done for the party at the compound salon; her father was at work, hoping to be able to get back in time to see the candles blown out. "Living the dream" is how David described it and chided me for not allowing us this same lifestyle. I questioned how people who lived that way could ever leave an expat life. "Repatriation" would make an interesting theme for a reality TV series, if you ask me.

Head-hunted

During my eight-month separation from David, I used the occasional lonely night to do a little web research on possible job opportunities for myself in Riyadh. My career had been based in the UK voluntary and community sector for the past 10 years, particularly around issues of social regeneration and equalities. Although the upwards movement of my career had frozen at the point I became a mother – mainly due to my insistence on staying in roles that I knew suited part-time hours – I still enjoyed my work hugely. I remember complaining to a friend once what a workaholic my Dad was. Trying out some amateur psychology on me, he sagely made a comment about me needing to recognise where different people gain their identities from. All our identities are subject to many influences: childhood, culture, family, friends and work. My friend suggested that an important part of my Dad's identity was career success and to be skilled in the role of the breadwinner. It's a conversation that has returned to me many times. Since becoming a mother, the energy and thought I put into parenting my children have undeniably formed a vital part of my identity. I am proud that I gave birth to my two daughters at home, making a definite decision not to troop off to hospital, with its availability of epidurals, pethidine and C-sections. I take an equal strength from my decisions to spend a full year's maternity leave with my daughters, before returning to part-time work; David also reduced his working hours at that time, to spend a day a week being a child-carer. We've never prioritised money but have seen a lot of value in the way we chose to bring up our children. That said, my identity outside the family home and role of mother has been a veritable life-support machine to me since my world changed in June 2003. I couldn't foresee how I could be truly myself in Riyadh if I were solely the family child-carer, pot-washer, cook and general domestic "facilitator". I knew job-hunting in such a conservative country, in terms of gender and race, would not be easy but I still believed it was worth the effort.

I started by looking for charities and non-governmental, not-for-profit organisations in Riyadh. In the countries of the Indian subcontinent I had some experience of – India, Bangladesh and Sri Lanka – this type of organisation was fairly prolific, arising out of the immense poverty starkly evident in city slums, on every street corner and the moment you stepped out of the international airports. In short, it was everywhere and unlikely to be history any time soon. An energetic community activism also existed in these countries, establishing groups committed to social development, in my experiences. The difficulty in these countries would have been honing my search down to find the most relevant, efficient and well-regarded organisations in my field.

My difficulty when job-searching in Riyadh was finding *any* organisations working for social development goals. I will not pretend that I can offer an in-depth analysis of this situation. However, my superficial hypothesis would be that for a country as wealthy as Saudi Arabia is alleged to be, in theory there should not be any citizens experiencing deprivations such as poverty; inadequate housing, education, or health facilities, or lack of clean water. These are all pervasive issues in the Indian sub-continent. Moreover, there has been neither war nor natural disaster in Saudi Arabia for generations, so there are none of the redevelopment issues that Sri Lanka is experiencing following the 2004 Boxing Day tsunami, added to decades of civil war. There were indisputably disparities in wealth in Saudi Arabia, but I was told that the oil wealth *was* distributed. For example: Saudi nationals received money on marriage and the births of their children. Although there were rumours that the burgeoning branches of the Saudi royal family were bleeding the coffers dry, on paper at least, the country could afford to provide decent education, health and other such services for its people. Thus, in theory, no one should be in need. Of course, there were other social issues that a Westerner such as me could see warranted addressing: the education of females; introducing the idea of religious, gender and ethnic tolerance; widening the Quran-based curriculum in state schools; encouraging young people to learn the skills necessary to the future of the economy, such as engineering or international law. There appeared to be no organisations working to these aims. Again, my superficial hypothesis would be that such organisations would not be permitted to start up or operate.

During my job-search, I identified the United Nations at the top of my rather short wish-list of potential employers. After arriving in Riyadh, I heard about a local breast cancer charity operating in the city. Both these organisations became the targets of my daily cold calls. Not daily because I wanted to promote myself as tenacious, but because I had to make numerous calls simply to navigate my way through the Arabic-speaking central switchboard system. Each time I called, I used to randomly press a button between 1 and 9 whenever there was a pause in the recorded voice, hoping that this would be the time I would get through to a real person. My parents criticise my stubbornness but sometimes it works in my favour. I not only located a real live human being but, following several red herrings and dead-end numbers, one week later had secured myself interviews at both organisations, subject to them approving of the details on my CV. In the UK, I used to advise community groups on equal opportunities-based recruitment processes. Clearly, I was not about to embark on such a process here. There was no specific vacancy advertised and CVs were required – both details that would have horrified me if I'd heard about them in UK. When in Rome, as they say…

My first interview was at the breast cancer charity. By then I owned a range of abeyas for my Saudi life: elegant, clean one; cheap, everyday one; dusty one with a tattered hem, saved for picnics at the wadi and other outdoor family activities, such as digging for fossils or quad-biking. I chose to wear the elegant one and gave no thought to the clothes under it. Big mistake. I walked through a doorway into the charity's office, labelled with a sign declaring, "Women only". On arrival I found myself surrounded by Saudi women not swathed in abeyas but instead in head-to-foot designer office wear: sharp suits, killer heels, immaculate white shirts. The women-only inner sanctum of the breast cancer charity's office permitted the shedding of the abeya. The staff were so glamorous, with tumbling locks, flawless make-up and manicured hands. My make-up regime consists of me choosing which bhindi to put on that day. I racked my brains, trying to remember if I had brushed my hair that morning. A kind assistant waited patiently to take my abeya. I experienced my first ever reluctance to shed it because it covered the too casual sarong and vest top lurking underneath. This snazzy get-up was fine for compound life but totally out-of-place here. Thus I had my first "learning episode" regarding job-hunting in Riyadh – smart interview clothes must always be worn. I took off my abeya amidst painful apologies. I went bravely into the interview, daring to hope that the substance of the woman would outweigh the cut of her cloth.

The charity had been set up by a Saudi princess and was managed by a vibrant, confident Saudi woman. Together we identified potential work she could offer that I could apply my skills to. The sticking point came when I brought up the subject of working hours. Even though I had knowingly entered a selection process not guided by equal opportunities, I thought I would still chance it by asking about part-time working. My daughters' school day ended at 1pm and the childcare available in Riyadh was not suitable for me or my children. The CEO seemed more shocked at this request than at my attire. Her argument roughly went: "If I had a husband lenient and liberal enough to *allow* me to work, why would I not want to grab the opportunity of a career and work full-time?" She, like most of the other staff, had children plus a full-time nanny or two at home for childcare. The part-time working hours I could offer – mornings only – were also not very useful in a country where life seemed to really get going for local people after lunch and continued late into the night. Any networking, training, events and so on would have been scheduled much later in the day than the 8.30am to midday slot I tentatively offered. Unsurprisingly, no job offer was made. My work/

life balance objectives proved a "deal-breaker".

Onwards and upwards to interview number two at the UN. I was better prepared this time and wore a suitable interview outfit underneath my abeya. At the breast cancer charity's office abeyas could be removed as we were in an all-women environment. The UN building in Riyadh is a mixed-gender environment, but it is located in the Diplomatic Quarter, which is somewhat confusingly regarded as an international no man's land, where the usual Saudi rule of abeya-wearing is temporarily suspended. The international airports in Saudi Arabia have this same status. I was interviewed by a mid-level manager, who was Egyptian. He would have been my line-manager. My astonishment was truly profound when he listened calmly to my request for part-time, school-hours working, then told me how much he admired my stance. I lifted my jaw off his desk after a couple of seconds, as I felt it might undermine my professionalism somewhat. He agreed to my request, going so far as to tell me that he believed that someone like me would probably achieve a full day's work in my morning hours. I was on Cloud Nine for days after this. Working for the UN – albeit as a "local hire" on local wages – offered an amazing experience for my career and life in general. The enforced career break that I had dreaded that my Riyadh years would comprise, would instead deliver me an unexpected opportunity to learn new skills and gain an insight into the international development field. I didn't just virtuously think about my career development. I couldn't help myself swaggering about a bit, imagining the impression I would make on my former colleagues and manager in UK, when I wrote to ask for a reference to be sent to the UN in Riyadh.

David was equally over the moon and the two of us went round telling everyone on the compound and at his work about my new job. My Appachi (paternal grandmother) was very superstitious and used to warn us of "*kanuru*", which roughly translates from Tamil as "the evil eye". You attract kanuru by having too much pride in yourself and boasting too much. I practically opened the door to our villa and invited kanuru in at this point in my life. One week later, I was on the phone to my new boss, trying to firm up a start date. He apologetically told me the offer was withdrawn. He was really sympathetic and regretful but his hands were tied. When my details got to the HR Department at the UN, including my part-time working request and his agreement to it, it was rejected. The protocol was for full-time positions only and there was to be no further discussion. I thrive on discussion however, so set about trying to negotiate, by offering to work for three months on probation for no wage, so my effectiveness could be assessed. However, the HR department proved more than a match for me; it refused to deviate from its protocol; even volunteers had to work full-time hours. I hit the ground with a thud and crawled around in a pit of anger, self-pity and misery for over a week. This cheery state of affairs was exacerbated by constantly bumping into fellow residents who inevitably, and thoughtfully, asked when my new job would start and commented on how excited I must be. Here was my second "learning episode" in the etiquette of job-hunting in Riyadh: do not tell anyone anything in relation to job-hunting, interviews or job offers – except your partner – until you have actually started in post. Ideally, I would recommend waiting for your first month's pay check before you tell anyone about a potential job.

I took a break from job-hunting in the inflexible, cruel outside world and decided to create my own job. I had been a yoga devotee for over 10 years and needed my weekly class almost as much as my Friday night large glass of red. Two other residents ran step and aerobics classes, but there were no yoga classes. I was told classes were available on a compound about 40 minutes away, which had a good reputation, but they were right in the middle of the afternoon, seemingly targeted at expat women without children or expat mothers with nannies. I was neither. Thus, I decided to begin "guided yoga practice sessions". I was wary of calling them yoga classes outright as I am not a qualified yoga teacher – something I made explicitly clear in my marketing. Being sued for yoga malpractice by a resident would have been the final straw for me right now. The compound allowed me to use the dance studio in our community centre – absolutely ideal, with its wooden floors and mirrors on three sides. As long as my classes were only open to residents, they would not charge me for use of the space. This was really valuable as for the first three months I ran the classes free of charge. Later on, as no one got broken after an hour's "guided yoga practice" with me and good word spread, I was increasingly asked by non-residents if they could attend, particularly fellow members of my running club. I always had to regretfully turn them away. The compound management made it very clear that if non-residents began coming to my classes, they would charge me for hire of the space. Although I did start charging for my classes, in line with the aerobics and step classes, I would not have been able to consistently afford to pay the compound rates for the studio hire. This was done deliberately: the compound owner, like most other owners around the city, wanted to ensure the compound facilities were only used by its residents. I even heard of a compound that did not allow residents to invite "outside" friends over to join them for pool-side time. This was a common weekend activity for us during the summer, as the two families we most enjoyed spending time with lived on other compounds. I have many good memories of all our children playing together whilst we talked on a range of topics that had absolutely nothing to do with other fellow residents, or any other minutiae of compound life. There were some people on the compound who only socialised with other residents, even holidaying with other residents. This was not appealing to either David or me. In fact, if our lifestyle there *had* developed in such an insular way, my mental health would have been even more challenged than it already was.

Leaving compound bureaucracy behind us, I loved teaching yoga in Riyadh. I have an Adult Education Teaching Certificate, gained during my time as a manager and trainer at an education resource centre in UK. I enjoyed using those skills in a completely different way, to plan yoga classes that encompassed total beginners to yoga-savvy students who were easily on the same level as I was. I started off running one evening class a week, before being cajoled into running a second, daytime class. I say "cajoled" because my morning, child-free hours were like gold dust to me. I used all the available time I had after trudging through the monotony of household tasks – such as the laundry and cooking meals specially designed to make my children grimace – to study my law course. Eventually, I was running three classes a week – two in the evening and one in the daytime, all on a drop-in, pay-as-you-go basis. In addition to this, I taught the occasional private one-to-one class, for which I charged a higher fee.

I scheduled the classes around my children's timetable in such a way that I was not affected by David's many business trips away. My daytime class was sometimes not possible during school holidays, but I was often able to beg an hour's childcare swap with another mum. My evening classes were timed just after my daughters' bedtimes, so I could put them to bed and zip down to the dance studio on my trike – barely a three-minute journey – with a babysitter in situ. I remember an episode from my previous work-life: during a regional conference, I was admonished by a Government Office staff member for being "parochial" regarding an issue I was lobbying for. I laughed to think how much more parochial I became in Riyadh – all my work was based within the walls of the compound I lived on, providing services only to my fellow residents, whom I saw frequently on a day-to-day basis. I also ran the weekly Children's Library, where I spent more time with the young children, their mothers and nannies of the compound. At least my yoga evening classes were fairly mixed, with some men and women attending whom I never saw during the day. I just about managed to keep my "boundaries" and relationships healthy with the aid of my anti-social behaviour – immersing myself in my studies all day. This meant I did not go on the shopping bus or attend coffee mornings, or any of the other daytime activities that many of the female residents did together.

I loved the job I had created for myself for so many reasons. I felt pride – remaining ever vigilant for kanuru – in being known around the compound as "the yoga teacher", rather than Shivani and Riya's mum or David Nicholls' wife. I found it virtually impossible to get anyone to use the word "partner" in Riyadh, which is how David and I describe each other. I advertised my classes via our email distribution network, but my marketing was helped hugely by my students' good word-of-mouth. Some students even came three times a week. I took all this as really positive and affirming feedback, vital to me in a country and social situation that threatened to take away much of my identity, self-confidence and skills. I don't think the people who attended my classes ever realised how much they helped me be able to bear living in Riyadh. When I left in June 2011, teaching my last ever class was one of the "farewell episodes" I put off for as long as possible.

I have always been fiercely committed to having my own financial independence. One of the many reasons I know that David's the right partner for me is because he has no qualms in telling people that during the early years of his mature apprenticeship with Rolls Royce, I was our main earner. The decision to come to Riyadh included me contemplating the idea of not financially contributing to our family for the first time ever – and I really struggled with it. So I am not ashamed to admit to also enjoying earning my own small pot of money through my classes. I used to joke that I was hoarding a "run-away fund" to enable me to buy my own plane ticket out of there if ever necessary. In reality, I appreciated taking David out to dinner for his birthday and paying the bill myself; meeting my own expenses for the perennial yoga and running gear I needed; and giving the family a trip to watch horse-racing, "tickets on me".

One item that was "on" David's employer was sponsorship of my law studies. Part of David's package included a "Partner Education Allowance". During our period of quandary over whether David should take the Riyadh job, we had identified this pot of money equally as a carrot to get me out there, and a lifejacket for the possible turbulent times ahead of me. My career, although not particularly high-flying, was nevertheless vitally important to me. I relished my paid work even more after motherhood entered my life – for the skills I used, the feedback I got and the challenges it offered. For some time, I had been interested in studying law in more depth than the occasional one-day training course I went on through work. Moreover, there was a gap in the voluntary and community sector, where I worked, for people with grassroots experience in the sector in addition to legal knowledge pertinent to the sector. David's new job and our move to Riyadh gave the perfect opportunity for me to take a career break, study a law course and make use of the "Partner Education Allowance" in David's contract.

I will always be grateful for the chance I got to study law in a focused and intense way. It's unlikely that I would have been able to do something like this when we were back in UK – where both of us juggled jobs, two children and a few life-supporting hobbies of our own. Compound life and the girls' school hours entirely suited part-time studies. I had less than minimal interest in going to coffee mornings, getting on the morning shopping bus, or learning golf – some of the other diversions available to me. Even better, my studies always gave me a valid excuse not to do these activities so, hopefully, I didn't appear totally churlish and anti-social to others. There was always an essay I was working on, or an exciting new unit that needed my full concentration. As the mother of daughters, I believe that I am a role model for them as females. Having paid work outside the family is important to me partly for the message that it sends to Riya and Shivani about the aspirations they can have. David and I were always very clear that my law course was one of my jobs in Riyadh. I was thrilled when the girls asked to have some old books they could use as law books: they liked to underline sentences in pencil and make notes in the margin, just as they saw me do in my own law books.

On Thursday afternoons, David would usually take the girls to the pool on his own. Whenever I had child-free time, once the ubiquitous household tasks were dealt with, I studied. In the beginning, David and the girls used to be quizzed about why I wasn't there. Part of the fabric of compound life is seeing a mother on her own with her children, but if the children's father is out with them solo, this is more unusual and questions will be asked. Eventually the message got through; David and our daughters consistently and contentedly told people that I was working, studying my law course. On the rare Thursday afternoons when I did venture out with the rest of my family to the pool, some people would come and offer me unnecessary sympathy regarding the onerous demands of my law studies. The truth of the matter was that I chose not to join them. We always spent Thursday mornings together, in an "off- compound" activity; Thursday afternoons were Daddy-time. I felt my daughters had to spend far too much time with me and that it was really important for them and David to have time together, away from me.

I still hadn't completely given up the idea of trying to do some kind of work beyond the compound walls. I particularly wanted the chance to work amongst Saudi people. Expat, compound life with young children does not lend itself well to meeting and befriending Saudis. The conservative culture in the country exacerbated this situation. Being seen as a potentially corrupting Western influence by some obviously does little to foster cross-cultural friendships. I looked back at the number of Bangladeshi friends my parents had had during their years in Dhaka and felt a pang of regret and guilt. Shivani had one Saudi classmate whom she became good friends with. In turn, her mother and I became friends too. I learnt a little about Saudi life during the occasional weekend morning we spent together at her villa, whilst our children all played together with the multitude of toys and entertainment equipment on hand there. However, I felt a little uncomfortable to have one token Saudi friend during my years in Riyadh. It smacked of the tokenism I used to warn nurseries and childminders against during my years as an early years equalities trainer, when they used to tell me that they had one black doll available for the children to play with.

My yoga teaching seemed to offer me a route off the compound. I met a group of Saudi women at a sculpture exhibition by a Saudi female artist. This was hosted at the villa of a female friend of the artist's, who had set up a travel agency providing tours within the country for expats. Whenever I was asked if I was working in Saudi, "I'm a yoga teacher" was my stock answer. The women were immediately interested. Thus began a long-winded process, carried out via email, of me trying to set up a weekly class for them, in the ideal conservatory space of this villa. An Arabic term much used in Saudi is "shway, shway" – translating roughly as "no rush". As an achievement-orientated, highly organised person, I failed miserably at "shwaying" and simply gave up emailing after about six weeks.

The second possibility that arose to teach yoga off the compound seemed more promising. This time, I was recommended for the post by a working female friend on the compound with royal connections. Luthan Hotel is the sole women-only hotel in Riyadh. It was set up, owned and funded by a Saudi princess, with a cadre of employees to manage its day-to-day operations. It's a beautiful place – a boutique hotel with a spa and gym attached. All of Luthan's facilities are predominantly frequented by very rich Saudi women; if they are not princesses themselves, then, at the least, they are connected to royalty. In theory, the new Spa Manager was head-hunting *me* but the process was so shambolic, I ended up taking over. I was asked to come for an interview but given no date or time. I think the idea was that I would just turn up that day and hang around until she could see me. This was totally out of the question so I sent her an email including a couple of suitable dates but got no response. When the first date and time on my proffered list arrived, I received a phone call, asking me why I wasn't at the interview. I explained that my email had requested that she confirm which date she had selected. "Oh. Did I forget to do that?" she asked. I held my tongue, tempted to ask whether I was better off lending my skills as a PA than as a yoga teacher. Putting this behind us, I managed to set up an interview with the Manager, an aristocratic Lebanese woman well- versed in the art of "shway, shway". My original email had made clear the available times I could teach – mornings only. I knew this kind of time would not be a good fit to the times Luthan's gym and hotel users would want classes. They were mainly Saudi women, living the Saudi hours that excluded early mornings but extended late into the night. The Manager hadn't fully digested that part of my email so was rather struck dumb when I re-clarified this information during the interview. Scheduled exercise classes usually took place during the late afternoon, from around 4pm, continuing up to around 9pm, when clients tended to return home for dinner or an evening of browsing malls and eating out. I was already teaching two classes a week in the evenings on the compound, which I was firmly committed to continuing, and was not overly keen to teach any more evening classes, particularly from 9-10pm, as seemed to most suit Luthan's clients. The hotel was a 30-minute drive from the compound, during a quiet spell. However, there is never a lull in the traffic in Riyadh at night-time. Considering that my alarm clock rang at 5.45am on weekdays to get the children ready for school, I believe this would have been described as burning the candle at both ends. The rich Saudi clientele doubtless had an army of nannies and maids who covered inconvenient tasks like the making of packed lunches and supervision of children's teeth-cleaning, whilst they had a well-deserved lie-in after their excesses of gym, yoga and spending serious cash at the mall the night before. I came to that now-familiar impasse regarding my available working hours and childcare principles.

Luckily for my daughters, another issue cropped up that gave a valid reason for Luthan not hiring me. I say "luckily" as otherwise the poor darlings would have had to endure another period of me stomping round the house and glowering accusingly at them, as I did after the UN disappointment. Again, as stated in my original email, I had made clear that I was not a qualified yoga teacher. In the UK, this would have definite ramifications on a gym's insurance. Once again, the Manager took this information in at the interview, as if for the first time. I suggested that the hotel look into the issue. I also thought the Manager should consider the impact on the other class instructors, all of whom I knew came to the job from other countries and held relevant formal qualifications from their homelands, such as New Zealand or South Africa. On top of it all, the gym had a reputation to protect with its very elite clientele. From a personal point of view, I thought I could be put into an uncomfortable and difficult position if a demanding customer queried my credentials to teach yoga. I frequently talked about escaping Saudi. However, I really didn't want to be suddenly dispatched from the country, with my iqama revoked at the instigation of an irate Saudi princess with a sore back after one my classes. I knew from a couple of anecdotes that being forced to leave the country with minimal notice can and did happen, if you had the misfortune to get on the wrong side of a well-connected Saudi in your line of work. I heard of an expat engineer who had worked in Riyadh for 17 years and counted it as his home. He had to leave the country with barely 48 hours' notice after making a number of comments on a project that a particularly sensitive senior Saudi colleague did not agree with. Unfortunately, his colleague had enough *wasta*[5] to have his iqama revoked, meaning he could no longer stay in the country. There was nothing that his employer – a Western multinational – could do about the situation. Evidently, they did not have enough *wasta* – and I was under no allusions how much David and I had.

A combination of all these issues – all flagged up in my original email – resulted in a very sweet phone call to me the next day from the Manager: she had so enjoyed meeting me, but felt Luthan could not take me on at this time. She told me to feel free to apply to them again in the future, if I became formally qualified in yoga. It was on the tip of my tongue to remind her that I hadn't actually applied to them in the first place, *they* had got in contact with me; I swallowed this down. Frankly, I was astounded to get the phone call at all, not just silence and the abrupt end of our communications.

Luthan Hotel's attempts at head-hunting me were pallid compared to some of the immediate and forthright attempts to employ me as a maid and nanny, initiated by Saudi women. These were partly fuelled by my ethnicity: most Sri Lankan women in Riyadh are there working

---

5   means power and influence – a highly important asset in Saudi life. Western expats generally have none of their own; they must rely on the of their connections.

as maids and nannies. My decidedly non-glamorous appearance did not dispel these perceptions either. The unexpected job offers made to me for this type of work usually arose in shopping malls and supermarkets, when I was with my daughters. The most memorable occasion occurred when I was walking through a mall food court with Riya and Shivani. I was helping them read the signs of the various food outlets, quizzing them about the type of food they thought would be served at each place. I became aware, from the movement of their bodies, that a trio of Saudi women were observing us. They were completely swaddled in black; even their eyes were barely discernible behind the black gauze of their niqabs. They clutched oversize takeaway cups of coffee with black gloves.

"You leave your employer. Come to work for me," a voice from behind one of the black shrouds was urging me. For the first time in my life, I found myself in an impromptu job interview with a face-less person I could not have any eye contact with; I struggled a little. The proposal was for me to work for this family as a nanny and to teach their young children to speak English. They were full of admiration for my English-speaking skills. Accepting the compliment, I explained in the little Arabic I knew that these were actually my daughters. They thought it was wonderful that I loved my employer's children like my own. This generosity of feeling I showed made them more determined that I should work for them. "Come and you will love my children too!" The truth finally hit them when Shivani and Riya encircled me, hugging me around my abeya, wailing, "This is *our* Mama. Don't take away *our* Mama!" The women seemed to think the entire episode was hilarious, and left still chuckling about it, with no apology offered to me and my daughters for their disruption. I soothed my soggy-cheeked children and picked my pride off the floor. It was only later that I realised I'd missed a golden opportunity by not enquiring about the employment package on offer. It would have been valuable to be able to tell David and the girls my current market rate for all the work I did for them for free.

Coffee mornings

Whilst I chose to bury myself in my law studies during every available child-free hour, there were other women on the compound who had a crammed social life. I sometimes emerged from my study, Quasimodo-like, after completing an assignment, to have a break by undertaking a social foray on the shopping bus. I once sat next to an effervescent resident, with grown-up children back in UK, who confessed that she returned home for a rest – her social life on the compound was so busy. Unfortunately for me, my achievement-orientated nature simply couldn't let me enjoy the social life and pastimes available to me on the compound.

Every month, various compounds hosted coffee mornings. These were open to all expat women in the city. Given the security situation on expat compounds in Riyadh, in addition to purchasing a ticket for the event, you also had to notify the event organiser in advance of your name, iqama number and which passport you held. Spontaneously deciding to attend one of these events was out of the question. Sometimes the coffee morning featured a speaker; make-up professionals seemed to have a regular slot. As a given, there was lots of food – cakes and pastries, as well as Middle Eastern fare such as olives, hummus and flatbreads – and usually stalls, selling pirate DVDs, jewellery, homemade produce such as jams or cakes and cheap abeyas. So, rather like the stereotype of a WI event, with the sale of cheap abeyas an unexpected bonus.

For those without a full-time driver at their disposal, getting to and from coffee mornings was done on the "shopping bus". The phenomenon of the shopping bus was available on most expat compounds. These were usually minibuses and provided a free service for residents. In the only country left in the world where women are not permitted to drive, shopping buses were a means of buying your groceries, getting new school clothes for your children and picking up gifts from the souk for people back at home. Our compound shopping bus went to a different destination every morning and afternoon, six days a week. The morning bus left after school drop-offs and returned around noon, before the end of the school day. The afternoon bus went at 4pm, when the shops reopened after the long afternoon closure. The bus timetable was sent out at the beginning of the month and residents could nominate different destinations in advance.

The "Second Hand" souk was a favourite request before Christmas. This was the souk where all the discarded finery of rich Saudi women was taken after they had become "last season". The souk was like a chaotic, open-air jumble-sale, never to be contemplated during the hot summer months. I returned from there with filthy feet, dusty eyes, bursting bladder (no toilets on site) but arm-loads of bargain-basement-priced, flamboyant dresses for me, my daughters and as gifts for most of my other female relatives. My mother and mother-in-law were both sent full-length evening dresses for their birthdays one year. I encouraged them to just wear them down to the local pub; they had only cost me about £2 so there was no need to keep them for "best". There's no order at the Second Hand souk so you have to be prepared to rifle through a range of different clothing. Gaudy dresses verging on the pornographic – designed to show both front and bottom cleavage in a decidedly un-Islamic fashion – nestled next to jewelled kaftans and flouncy Disney princess dresses. I bought amazing fake-fur-lined, embroidered coats for David and me, which he excitedly remembered being worn by local people in Uzbekistan. One lucky shopper rooted out a designer evening gown, of the type usually resplendent on a celebrity at Oscars' night, but without its usual price tag.

Some female residents used the shopping bus to socialise: they could get off the compound, chat on the bus with their friends and browse shops together, regardless of whether they needed to buy anything. The journey back was usually very upbeat and cheerful, with people showing each other their purchases, or sharing out titbits they'd just bought. The noise levels were pretty high, too. I once made

David come on the shopping bus so he had a first-hand experience of it. He got off the bus back at the compound, with a dazed expression on his face and a ringing in his ears. He had been overwhelmed by the voice levels and the fact that some people barely seemed to draw breath, they were talking so much. David rather rudely opines that I and all my family members have our volume buttons turned off; "loud Tamil voices" is the term he uses. As far as he was concerned, the whole bus was made up of "loud Tamil voices". A male resident on the shopping bus was a rare occurrence, so he had found himself a particular target to be included in conversations or have his opinion sought on purchases. I was highly amused; I had never heard David's views on cushion covers before.

There were plenty of activities available within the compound walls, too. In residence in the café on Wednesday afternoons was a dominoes club, who indulged in three-hour-long games. Bridge and Mah-jong sessions were available. Small groups of friends set up book clubs together. One particular book club member once admitted to me that the selected book was often ignored as the group members chatted about every other topic available over coffee and homemade cakes. For those with itchy fingers, there was a craft group, where members shared their skills in quilting, painting, knitting and so on. For a lot of residents, our compound being home to a nine-hole golf course was too good an opportunity to miss. You could either brush up on your game or learn it via the instructors who worked there. If you needed to work off the coffee morning calories, there were exercise classes run by some of the residents. In addition to my yoga classes, you could "go for the burn" in body conditioning, step aerobics or circuit training. Just before I left Riyadh, a trained Zumba teacher arrived on the compound – although, of course, this proved no solace for my devoted yogis. Personal trainers were also spotted working one-to-one with residents in the gym or around the compound.

There was always cooking for your family, "your man", or coffee mornings to devote some of the day's hours to. I found myself a reluctant captive audience at a family picnic event once, to a woman who regaled me with the saga of food shopping and cooking for her family in Riyadh. Her children and husband did not like the cakes available here – as I was told – so she did lots of baking during her child-free hours. Certain ingredients like marzipan were elusive, allegedly, so she had a "network" of friends who bought it for her whenever they chanced upon it. Frankly, if either my daughters or partner had reported a dislike of local shop-bought cake, I would have done the reverse of Marie Antoinette and let them eat bread.

In UK, David and I had shared the cooking 50/50. In Riyadh, the split was more like 10/90; and I found it a largely monotonous task, closely rivalled by that other daily requirement – the making of packed lunches for the three other family members. David is not a domineering, sexist partner. He never asked me to take on these or any other household tasks, but I felt some kind of ethical duty to do so, as I wasn't contributing financially to our family any more. The woman-who-baked-lots-of-cakes may have felt under this same obligation.

Whilst back in UK, our sharing of making the meals was not a rare phenomenon amongst our "couples friends". It would certainly have been in Riyadh. Only a minority of the men took their turn at cooking. More often, I heard comments like, "My husband has never touched a saucepan our whole married life". A few women told me they couldn't come to my evening yoga classes because that was the time their husbands returned from work – tired, hungry and needing their dinner. It was rather reminiscent to me of my young children's needs at 5pm every day. However, Riya and Shivani were always keen to get into the kitchen, to soak themselves in foam in the name of washing-up, or to saw cheese with a plastic knife to put in omelettes. Some husbands seemed to regard it as a "droit de seigneur" never to step foot into that area of their homes.

My flute teacher in Riyadh was also a Duke of Edinburgh leader. This involved her taking groups of teenagers into the desert for weekend hiking and camping trips. She described to me a regular occurrence she was confronted with over the years. When some of the teenage boys were told they were on rota to warm up that night's stew or pot of beans, there was a horrified reaction. "That's women's work!" There was stalemate until my friend, in humiliation, called in the male camp leader for back-up. You wouldn't have to search hard to find the male role models for those kinds of attitudes amongst expat and Saudi men alike.

The little compound café provided a take-away service which made a healthy profit from many of the single men on the compound. You could ring from the internal compound phone provided in each villa, place your order and even have the food delivered to you – even though the café was not more than five minutes' walk away from most villas. It was exactly like hotel room service, without the good excuse of being on holiday. During the eight months David lived alone in our villa, he never ordered from the café. Instead, he used to make big pots of lamb curry or spaghetti bolognaise a few times a week for his dinners. He said it gave him something to do after work, when he returned to the quiet, lonely villa. He also used to sometimes invite other single work colleagues over for dinner at the weekends. This set him apart from most of the other single men on the compound, whose voices and regular orders were known by the café waiters the moment they picked up the phone. "Good evening, Mr Sven. It's Monday night – so the Singapore noodles with extra chilli as usual?"

*   *   *

I wasn't the only female resident who made no time for any of the daytime compound activities "for ladies". A minority of the women worked, thus were not seen that often around the compound during the day. Most working mothers had jobs at one of the private, expat schools. There was a range in Riyadh, catering for the diverse expat communities: French, German, American and British schools were available. There were also other private schools, such as the Montessori school Riya, my youngest daughter, went to. Jobs available at these schools included teaching, working as a teaching or learning support assistant and administrative roles. Working at a school was compatible with your own children's school hours and holidays. Like me, most expat women on our compound were there through their partner's job. In UK, David and I had had jobs of a commensurate wage and grade. There was no question of me always having to take annual leave to cover school holidays, or always being the one to leave work for a sick child. We shared those responsibilities. However, in Riyadh, the situation was totally different. Mothers, or nannies, were the ones who covered childcare needs; any sharing of duties with fathers was for weekends only. That precious weekend time was frequently reduced to a Friday; many men worked on a Thursday. Moreover, I was by no means unique in having a partner often away on work trips; this was a common symptom of expat jobs in Riyadh.

At a point when my studying routine seemed to be making a morose hermit of me, I decided I should try something different. Riya's school was on the compound so I preferred not to volunteer there; I wanted to venture beyond our walls. Shivani's school didn't endear itself to me – although all her teachers were wonderful, I found the school too business-like and regimented. The private international school I ended up volunteering at – with the help of a compound acquaintance – was far more haphazard and flexible. I was allowed to choose my hours and the age range I wanted to work with. I worked as a volunteer Learning Support Assistant for a term, working one-to-one with 16-18 year olds.

Some of my students were a joy to work with – motivated and interesting, but needing support because they had dyslexia or other learning issues. What caused me to stop volunteering there were the students who struggled with no apparent learning need aside from being bored and spoilt. With my students with "genuine" support needs, I did extra work, focusing on their areas of weakness, such as structuring essays or improving grammar. With my least favourite group of students, I was told I had to help them do their homework, as they weren't getting it done at home. One teenage Saudi girl I worked with, Hania, appeared to be so used to maids around her, responding to her every need, that she was too lazy to even use the mouse while I attempted to help her finish off an overdue piece of art coursework on the computer. Another Learning Support Assistant whispered that the watch Hania had on was the latest "must-have" in the celebrity magazines and cost around $2,000. While helping Hania on an essay, yet again overdue, I learnt a bit more of her life. I was left, not envying her $2,000 watch, but feeling sorry for her.

Hania and her mother were the "first" family of her father (polygamy is permitted in Saudi Arabia). His second wife – very astutely – produced sons, so the father favoured this family more, living with them most of the time. He spent the occasional night at Hania's home during the week and every other weekend there. The essay Hania was working on was titled "Free time". Trying to ferret out information about how she spent her free time, to help her write her essay, revealed a rather lonely and monotonous life. Her home was filled with expensive gadgets and equipment – X boxes, Wii games, satellite TV – but, once back from school, Hania was pretty much trapped inside there with no company other than maids and her mother. The house had an outdoor pool Hania claimed never to have gone in. She was quite overweight, so was perhaps self-conscious of wearing a swimming costume. She couldn't ride a bike and said there was nowhere to ride one, anyway. Her house had no garden and she would not be allowed to ride a bike outside the villa walls. She wasn't allowed to go to friends' houses after school or invite them over to hers. Hania gave no reason for this, but I wondered whether it was because most of her classmates were non-Saudis, so too much interaction with their Western influences may not have been encouraged.

To illustrate this: a compound friend of mine taught English privately to a teenage Saudi girl. Her parents were liberal and allowed their daughter to come to the compound for English lessons. A good friendship developed between tutor and student; my friend was regularly invited over to the Saudi family's house for meals and to spend time. However, the parents confided to my friend that the friendship between her and their daughter had affected her marriage prospects. Being good friends with an English woman and regularly going to a Western compound were seen as indications of a young woman who may have been corrupted by Western influences. Many families would simply not want to marry a son to someone with that kind of stigma attached.

Hania and her mother were not allowed outside their villa unaccompanied; their outings were constrained to the times her father came to stay, when they would be taken out to malls and restaurants. The restricted life Hania was forced to lead seemed difficult enough to me without the added dimension of the long summer holidays. During the hot summer months, when schools were shut, the two families travelled to Europe together, often to Italy or Switzerland. There, they would live in a large rented villa together and Hania was allowed to live a different life. She told happy stories of relaxing at cafés, overlooking Italian piazzas, with her half brothers as chaperones; spending afternoons in parks by the lake in Geneva; and browsing boutiques for gorgeous clothes that would spend most of their time being either worn under an abeya or just within the walls of her home. To have regular forays into a more relaxed life with variety and choice, and then have to return to the Wahabi-ruled way of life in Riyadh, must place quite a stress on a person's mental and emotional states. Moreover, Hania was a teenager, going through all the usual hormonal upheavals of her age. It dawned on me why she lacked the motivation to do her homework. After graduating from this school, she might be permitted to continue further studies at the new all-women's university in Riyadh, but the odds were that she would not be able to seek a job or career after that. It seemed most likely that the long-term future held an arranged marriage and a life lived mainly in an opulent villa, punctuated by brief escapes to another lifestyle on holidays outside the Kingdom. I felt guilty about my original irritation with her, but equally felt unable to offer her sympathy, as that would have been inappropriate. All I could do was help her get her homework finished.

Race and racism

Which villa are you here to clean?" insisted the Saudi National Guard officer. Equally insistently, I repeated that I was a member of Riyadh Road Runners, there for today's race. The officer simply didn't believe me. He stubbornly refused to look at the list in his hand, with all the names of the registered runners for that day. With a surname beginning "Ba", my name usually appears pretty near the top of most alphabetical lists. The officer's sheaf of papers was tantalisingly near to me; I felt the urge to lean out of the taxi and grab them – to prove to him, beyond any doubt, that I was on the list. However, 18 months of living in Riyadh told me that that was a sure step to being point-blank refused entry or at least longer and more onerous detention at the security gate of this compound.

Let me explain this scene more fully to you. It was 6.30am on a Friday morning (the equivalent of a Sunday in UK). I had turned up at a compound in Riyadh, in a taxi from my own compound, to run a race with the Riyadh Road Runners, the expat-led running club I was a member of. It was such joy for me, to get up early on my own, in the still quiet and slumbering house, excitedly put my running gear and race number on, have a contemplative cup of coffee before picking up my sports bag and getting into a compound taxi, to be sped away to another compound somewhere else in the city. I would sit in the taxi, headphones on, and look out onto the deserted Riyadh streets. Some races took place on a compound quite far out of the city and I would be lucky enough to be driven past the camel souk, which was a strangely beautiful sight at that time of the morning – with black, brown and fawn-coloured camels of all sizes looking peeved with the new day already. At those precise moments, I wouldn't have swapped being anywhere else in the world. In this bubble of peace and happiness, I would arrive at my destination: where the troubles would start. It was not always a given, but too many times for it to be a one-off anecdote I would encounter problems getting unto the compound. The sticking point was centred in the unshakeable belief of the Saudi National Guard officer that I must be there as a maid to clean someone's villa, as I was obviously a Sri Lankan from my looks. The compound security guards, who tended to be from the Indian subcontinent, rarely helped. They similarly couldn't believe that a female of their ethnicity could be in Riyadh as anything other than a maid.

For people who have had the good fortune to never have lived behind walls topped with barbed wire, with security gates as the standard point of entrance, it will doubtless seem rather extreme to have two different types of guard to ensure your tranquillity and safety. This was the situation on most of the compounds which were home to non-Saudis in Riyadh. The multinational employers of these expats demanded that the compounds should be protected by the National Guard – the King's own army. This force is made up Saudi nationals and is intended to protect the ruling monarchy both from internal coups and external threats. They are trained and organised by a US defence consultancy, who have a whole compound to themselves in Riyadh. Guarding an expat compound was probably the fuzzy end of the lollipop for them – monotonous, unchallenging and probably an affront to their belief system. They were virtually never seen inside the actual compounds – where women wandered around at ease, abeya-less, or even jogged around in skin-tight sports gear, and residents took bottles of "moonshine" to the poolside for sundowners at weekends. If you were to go through the security gates at prayer time, the National Guard officers could be seen praying on prayer mats in the vicinity. I mused that if any terrorists had felt inclined to attack our compound, they need only time their strike during prayer time, when the National Guard officers were safely immersed in religious observance. The compound security guards were not armed so would not pose any real opposition in such a situation. They were usually from the Indian subcontinent, were never seen to break for prayer and appeared to work appallingly long shifts.

There are thousands of expats from the Philippines and Indian subcontinent in Riyadh, carrying out a wide range of manual jobs: drivers, gardeners, construction workers, maids, office cleaners. I use the word "expat" deliberately because a lot of people would differentiate: "expat" usually denotes the white-collar, very well paid Westerner, living on a compound; "foreign worker" tends to be applied to all the thousands of other non-Saudis, who literally keep the country going on a minimal wage. Iqamas were granted more readily to Muslims, hence the predominance of Bangladeshi gardeners and Filipino nannies. When you factor in the poverty often faced in their home countries, a three-year contract in Riyadh – with a regular wage higher than what was available at home – was like a child finding one of Willy Wonka's golden tickets. That precious package – iqama, contract and wage – demanded its pound of flesh, however. Construction workers continued working to build yet another flawless mall or prince's palace during the 48 degree Riyadh summer months. Maids and nannies worked a minimum six-day week, sometimes from 6am to 8pm. The compound taxi drivers rarely had a full day off. There was enough hardship without the added stresses that some of these workers had to endure, such as physical abuse, awful housing conditions or having their passports confiscated, tying them in to a working situation akin to indentured labour.

There are people in Riyadh from these countries who represented the other end of the foreign worker spectrum – they lived on Western, expat compounds; they had their own maids and drivers; and the men, in general, had lucrative contracts with large banks or multinational companies. However, due to the way I looked and dressed, I was rarely taken to be from these circles. The label most often attached to me when in Riyadh was that of a maid or nanny. On the one hand, I didn't mind the label. The majority of my day-to-day activities in Riyadh were indeed tasks often carried out by a maid or nanny. In UK, these tasks are simply those of running a home and bringing up a family: cooking, laundry, collecting your children from school or taking them to a friend's birthday party. On the other hand, I resented the treatment this label entailed, such as the arduous process of getting onto a compound for a race, or the barriers it put in my way, such as getting service I needed. On one occasion, I took Riya and Shivani to an open event at a new recreation facility at an embassy. With a bouncy castle, inflatable slide and face painting available, I knew the girls would be in heaven for a couple of hours. A cup of tea seemed a fitting reward for my supervision duties but I couldn't get served at the refreshment tent. The South Indian catering workers there thought I was someone's nanny – and the refreshments were available only to "diplomats", I was told. In other words, not for "workers" but "expats". In a fury, I spoke to the event's organisers and was duly served. Unfortunately, the treat of a cuppa now tasted bitter.

Even though it could have been easy to feel singled out for this kind of treatment, I knew my experiences were shared by numerous other non-white women. A Korean woman I met reported being unable to count the times people thought she was the nanny when out with her white English partner and mixed-race young son. A Peruvian woman at the embassy event consoled me in my fury and swapped stories of mistaken identity, of people believing she was her white American husband's Filipino maid.

My work history included time as an anti-racist trainer in UK, specialising in early years work. I do believe that it's valuable to talk openly about issues of difference and discrimination from a young age with children, and have done so with my daughters. However, I tried to shield them from these episodes. Firstly, I had my hands full of the task of championing gender equality at home. I didn't want to leave the sexist society of Riyadh with my precious, bright daughters harbouring doubts about their value in the world and aspirations they were allowed to have, as a result of the messages they were picking up about gender discrimination in this conservative, Islamic country. Secondly, regarding the episodes of racism from people who shared my ethnic heritage; it was so hard to explain why they themselves would discriminate against me. Didn't it actually make life harder for them? The caste system that continues to operate in the Indian subcontinent shoulders some of the blame. The caterers at the tea stall could not tolerate serving someone of their "caste", or social status; they were there to serve those of a higher rank: Western expats. An acquaintance told me a tale of her very rich, IT hotshot Indian friend not being able to get the Indian sales assistant in an expensive watch shop to serve him. He was only able to make his purchase when she accompanied him in; she's a white Central American woman.

This hierarchy from the Indian subcontinent was perpetuated in Saudi Arabia, where people were accorded different treatment due to their employment status – and therefore social status – in addition to the colour of their skin and religion. I had expected some kinship shown from Saudis towards Muslims of other nationalities, but was soon disabused of that idea. The Bangladeshi Muslim filling cars with petrol was foremost a manual worker of low status, best treated as invisible and definitely not as a "Muslim brother". Conversely, a white Western bank manager – and a closet Christian in a country where no reference or acceptance of any other religions was tolerated – was shown the utmost courtesy and respect. On the other hand, if that same bank manager were Western but of Indian ethnicity, he would not consistently be shown that same level of courtesy and respect. Emphasising his English or American accent and drawing attention to the MBA from a US university probably improved matters.

I cannot really continue without giving more detail about the intolerance extended towards other religions and ways of life by Saudi Arabian regulations. When David and I were packing up our house prior to our move, we spent an afternoon with a representative from the shipping company. He walked around our home, pointing out which items would be most likely not to get through Saudi customs. Obviously, that golden, promising bottle of malt whiskey we had been saving was a no go, and the oak-cured Wiltshire ham; but other, somewhat surprising items joined that list. All my books on world religions, mythology and world folk tales were consigned to the storage pile, to be boxed up and left in our loft before our tenants moved into our home during our extended absence. Although not a practising Hindu, I have a colourful and sentimental array of Hindu gods and goddesses around my home, mostly presents from family members. These had to be left behind, snugly wrapped in newspaper alongside all the homemade Christmas decorations the children had made at various playgroups and nurseries over the years. Any ornaments and artefacts linked with that blasphemous festive occasion of Christmas would not get through customs, advised the shipping representative. Worse than that: customs officials generally carry out random checks on boxes; finding contraband such as tinsel, plastic Christmas trees and inflatable Father Christmases in just one box would prompt them to thoroughly search every single other box in our shipping consignment, we were cheerfully told. Framed photos could be taken but a few paintings we had featuring figures of people had to be left behind: it is considered un-Islamic for a person to depict the human form; that is beyond the realm of mortals and to be left in the hands of divine beings.

On the subject of mortals, it is advisable not to declare any other religious belief than Islam or "none" on any official documentation related to entry to and residency in Saudi Arabia. I heard that admitting you were Jewish would automatically bar your entry to the country. Israel is not officially recognised to exist by Saudi Arabia. My brother cited the Israeli stamp in his passport, from backpacking days, as an opt-out clause for ever having to visit us in Riyadh, with rather obvious relief. Other factors would indisputably have hindered his entry into the country, anyway: his ethnicity. A young, single Sri Lankan man would have rung alarm bells as a potential illegal immigrant, seeking employment as a labourer or driver, despite his British passport, Cambridge degree and work as an economist. It proved a breeze to get a visitor's visa for David's mother to come and visit. Getting them for my parents was a different story. Despite evidence of their British nationality, the Riyadh civil servants responsible for approving their visas were highly suspicious that my parents were merely pretending to come to visit us. It seemed very probable to them that my parents would decide to forego returning to their comfortable, liberal lives in UK, where they had lived for around 30 years, owned their own home and had professional jobs, to stay in Riyadh, to be someone's driver and maid. Trying to assure these civil servants that this was one of the most unlikely events to ever happen in world history without either laughing in their faces, or being overtly critical of their homeland or using the term "pigs would fly", was a testing experience. After stringing out the racism and humiliation for as long as possible, my parents were finally granted visitors' visas. Unfortunately, these racist attitudes prevailed when we tried to get a visitor's visa for an aunt I am very close to, to spend a certain festive and family event around the middle of December with us. Like my parents and me, she also has dual nationality, with both Sri Lankan and British passports, and lives in Sri Lanka. The authorities this time could not be swayed in their view that she was attempting to sneak into the country, choosing to leave her beautiful, grand home, full-time cook, car and creative job behind her in Colombo to work illegally as a maid. I don't need to spell out that David and my mixed-race relationship was integral to these situations.

To finish my earlier story: I did eventually get unto the compound and to my race, despite my "race", as it were. Although to me, it felt that these episodes lasted for a good half an hour, it usually only took about 10 minutes of tenacity and infuriating repetition for the army officer to decide to humour me and glance at the running club list. Gradually making my English accent more and more like a splendid chap from a Jeeves and Wooster novel also oiled the wheels of the process. And behold! There was the name Baghirathan on the list, standing out like a sore thumb, and all was well. The security barrier went up, my taxi went in and I would always get over my rage and frustration by running it out of my system. It's important to say that I never encountered this issue when I went to events with David driving, or when I travelled there with other runners, generally white and male.

Keeping afloat

I love the Stevie Smith poem about someone in the sea – spotted by people on the beach – who's "not waving, but drowning". I worked hard in my Riyadh years to prove to everyone, including myself, that I was not drowning but waving. I fought a regular battle with bouts of very low self-esteem and feelings of loneliness. I often felt that my life was stuck in an unhealthy vacuum, whilst the rest of the family seemed to be thriving. I was there for the "greater good" of our family unit as a whole, but often felt a rather invisible, neglected part of that whole. However, it was not all doom and gloom, by any means. I am an energetic and motivated person, characteristics that were tried to new limits in Riyadh. My law studies were a vital anchor in the sea of compound life, but they did result in solitary mornings at home, in front of the computer, with law books spread out around me. This took some adjusting to, as my former job had entailed attending meetings and running training courses. I had often worked away from my desk, cycling to different locations around the city, to meet with a diverse range of people – local government officers, community activists, parents and older people. I worked as best as I could to adapt to my new life, but I know supporting my emotional needs was quite a drain on David.

I sought catharsis from other sources too. Running is a hobby I had grabbed at when motherhood became part of my life. It was an easy way to get out of the house and exercise, and the benefits to my state of mind proved even more valuable. It soon developed into the time where I cleared my head and rejuvenated my attitude. Shivani once said I was a "happier Mama" after a run. Ah: the wisdom of infants. Back in UK, I tried to do at least one half marathon a year to have a goal to train for. I was able to keep up my hobby in Riyadh through the local expat running club. Riyadh Road Runners was without doubt one of the best "happy pills" I took during my years in Saudi. I had been apprehensive at going along to one of their events, expecting an intimidating group of Lycra-clad elite athletes. Instead, I met open, warm-hearted, down-to-earth people, with a range of athletic abilities. There was relatively little to do in Riyadh, so the club attracted a mixed bag of expats, in relation to nationality, age and fitness. Without question, there were some inspiring, national-level runners, but there were also power walkers; teenage girls who strolled and chatted their way around the course; and, during my last club season, my young daughters joined the membership ranks and competed in the shortest races.

The Road Runners' season was from September to April – the cooler months of the Saudi year. Races of differing lengths – starting at 5km, peaking at marathon distance – took place every other Friday morning on compounds across the city. Arranging races on compounds meant that women could safely participate without wearing abeyas. The events were inclusive and accommodating; participants could run or walk and did not have to attempt the full distance. Half marathon takes me to the edge of my enjoyment of running, so David and I competed in the marathon as a team: I ran the first three loops of seven km, David the last three, at a sickeningly quicker time than I could ever dream of achieving.

David was a member of Riyadh Wheelers during our Saudi years – the local expat cycle club. His events took place on alternate Friday mornings to my running races. This was planned deliberately as many expats, particularly single men with lots of time to fill at weekends, were members of both clubs. David's events took place on public roads, on the edge of the city. Usually, the racing cyclists would be the only traffic out on these roads during their events – very early on Friday mornings, the Islamic holy day. However, when there were instances of cars appearing and driving alongside the cyclists – out of curiosity, mainly – I heard that the male cyclists would form a shield around the small minority of female cyclists, to protect them from inquisitive eyes. Dressed in the same Lycra suits as the men, with hair pulled back tightly under cycle helmets, it would be difficult for a suspicious driver to definitely report that he had seen a woman without an abeya on a bike. It's an anecdote that, for me, gives an example of a solidarity that was specific to being in Saudi, when individual athletes' aspirations to come first or to get a "PB" –personal best – became less of a priority than safeguarding all club members.

The gap in the Road Runners' calendar was neatly filled by the Riyadh Triathlon club, which David and I also joined. Every Friday from April to September, there was the mouth-watering opportunity to either participate in a biathlon (swim/run races), duathlon (run/cycle races) or full triathlon (swim/cycle/run). I chose the biathlons; David got the duathlons; so we kept harmony at home by continuing to take it in turns to slip gleefully out of the house in the early hours of Friday mornings to take part in a race. The full triathlons' registration time was 4.30am – which proved just that little bit too early, even for us.

Unsurprisingly, our athletic hobbies rubbed off on our daughters. In a way designed to infuriate me, Shivani and Riya absolutely refused to take up any of the children's activities available after school on the compound, such as tennis or ballet. I forgave their wilfulness a fraction when they declared that they wanted to run. Although the running club was my sanctuary, I simply couldn't ignore both daughters' enthusiasm. During my last club season I came to a compromise: my daughters took part in the short races – five km and five miles – where they chose how many one km or one mile loops they felt able to do. David is a very good runner but could usually never compete in Road Runners' events as he covered our childcare. So, through this compromise, he was able to compete seriously in the short races, whilst I jogged alongside Riya for a lap. Being the youngest competitor by far, Riya was allowed to take part on her scooter, keeping well out of the way of runners. After her first race, going slowly along with me and Riya, Shivani became confident and competitive enough to speed off on her own, seriously running a couple of laps before pulling off decent sprint finishes. I can report with pride that her time per mile was akin to my own during the last two torturous miles of a half marathon. The club really helped keep up the girls' motivation by making a big fuss of them. Their times were always included in the results table that was emailed out after each event. They had their own runner numbers for the season and extra small club T-shirts were specially ordered for them. They were cheered over the finish line like no-one else. Without doubt, the experience with Riyadh Road Runners was one of the most positive aspects of our family life in Saudi.

I couldn't help but notice how many of my fellow female residents had personal trainers, yet only a minuscule minority actually participated in athletics clubs such as Road Runners or the Tri Club. It was as if having the goal of sculpting one's abs, or losing that troublesome extra pound from coffee morning indulging was appropriate; whereas, getting out of one's comfort zone, to go to different locations around the city, to compete in a mixed gender environment was simply a goal too far for some. I pondered whether the gender segregated environment of Saudi Arabia influenced even expat women to feel more comfortable in all-women environments. On my compound, the personal trainers most used were a couple of female residents who had personal training qualifications from their home countries. Moreover, during the daytime, it was rare to see a male resident in the gym; this area was a de facto all-female environment during working hours.

Road Runners was made up of a majority of male runners. Most female members had come to Riyadh in their own right, through paid employment. Many were medical practitioners, some were teachers, and a few were civil servants. Their aspirations and daily routines already took them off compounds and into varied, mixed gender environments, so continuing that in their hobbies was probably not such a psychological leap as it may have been for other expat women who shared as curtailed a daily existence as I did.

The practicalities of participating in clubs may also have created a barrier. Generally, personal training sessions went on during the daytime, when partners and children were at work or school. Club races were early on Friday mornings – the Saudi Sunday – and, in the absence of my own personal driver, I always took taxis to them. Fridays tended to be the only day a week maids/nannies weren't asked to work, so childcare to participate in races would have to be covered by partners. In some family's cases, a father's absence on work trips was the status quo, rather than an occasional event. In more traditional families, asking for childcare from a spouse to be able to run round and round a compound may have been out of the question. My mother-in-law is an assertive woman; order her about at your own peril. Nevertheless, I remember her telling me that my partner and his twin brother were three years old before she left them with their Dad on their own. I suspect she had to promise to be back within the hour, too. I don't need to refer to statistics from the Fawcett Society to be confident that this traditional division of family roles has not died out in UK. In my recent history, since becoming a mother, I've listened with disbelief to men I had hitherto regarded as both sane and intelligent, seriously proclaiming that women's hands are better suited to changing nappies because "they are smaller than most men's hands". There seems no reason to doubt the sexist division of family roles is alive and kicking in the expat world, too.

I did have to miss a few races, with very bad grace, due to David being away on work. Bother that maid and her day off! However, there were many races I was able to participate in, despite David's absence, thanks to the generosity and consideration of other club members. Race marshals or those carrying out the timing used to keep an eye on Riya and Shivani for me on some occasions. This kind of set-up was only possible in a place like Riyadh, where the culture forced our races to take place on compounds, which were largely safe places for children to play with minimum supervision. I have a fond memory of doing a swimming time trial at the beginning of the Tri Club season, leaving my daughters to play in the spectator stands, with an infrequent eye kept on them by another participant's teenage daughter, Minnie. I wager the health and safety anxieties in UK, not to mention the need for CRB checks, would have impeded me doing this back in Bristol.

Initially, it was Road Runners as an entirety that was such an essential resource in my life in Riyadh. I went along alone in a taxi, regardless of which other runners I expected to encounter there. Although some of the club's elite runners – those always in the top 10 finishers – were frequently absorbed in technical conversations about training schedules for their next "Iron Man" or international marathon, most other runners were happy to chit-chat about anything, with anyone who came along. If my family didn't turn up for the post-race breakfasts, I sat happily at any spare space, knowing I would get into conversation with my neighbours within a minute. That's the unique connection and camaraderie arising from the madness of running around a compound in Riyadh, at an unsociable early hour on a weekend morning, often in oven-like heat. Having recently seen each other in utilitarian running gear, sweat-soaked and panting, broke down barriers of gender, class and ethnicity pretty effectively. It's hard to describe how much I loved this atmosphere, without coming across as a kind of evangelical obsessive. I am confident that some of my fellow residents avoided me on the compound on Friday afternoons, when I was brimming over with the joy of my morning race and social experience.

Over the course of my second season, there were certain characters I got to know better and whom I began to look forward to meeting up with. An American man, Dave, referred to himself as "my nemesis" because we were often neck-and-neck in races, constantly battling to get ahead of the other. I was always disappointed when he didn't appear for a race, and my finish time definitely suffered without him to compete against. Amy was an English woman who had never run before joining the club. At the beginning of the 2010/11 season, we often ran in the same pack; our times were pretty similar. However, she was so bitten by the running bug that she trained much more than me. Over the course of the season, I saw her lead on me growing by the race. I was gutted but begrudgingly excited for her. As part of David and my "exit strategy" from Riyadh, I signed us both up for the Swindon Half Marathon for October 2011. Amy and her family left Riyadh at the same time as us to relocate near Swindon. She also signed up for the 2011 Swindon Half, along with another club member who was also returning to UK. I was thrilled that I would be able to catch up with her there, although I knew that once the race started, all I would see would be her runner number on the horizon, spurring me on. We suggested to the club that the website and newsletter should begin to include a section featuring photos of members wearing their Riyadh Road Runners T-shirts, competing in events around the world. There were four club T-shirts on display at the Swindon Half in October 2011 to get the ball rolling.

A large personality in the club – and one of its founders – was a French man, Conrad. He was in his 70s and had lived in Riyadh from the time I came out of nappies. His wife had long given up on living there or trying to get him to leave. So he continued with the job he enjoyed and with his passion – running in Riyadh. He was always to be spotted up in the lead pack, but without fail he cheered on the runners like me, who doggedly brought up the rear. I had the privilege of him as a running partner in only one race. I was on the peak of my form but still only managed to keep up with him because he was recovering from a serious knee injury. He was charming in a way only an athlete could get away with: he told me it was more pleasant running with me than his usual pack, who were mainly men, because I smelt nicer. My sweet fragrance proved not enough of an incentive to keep him at my side at the next race, though.

Peter was another stalwart, in terms of longevity in Riyadh and with the club. My initial instinct was to keep out of his way, as his continual stream of banter was pretty misogynist and a red flag to my feminism. He was rather proud of his role of chauffeuring "Czech chicks" (as he called them) to different athletic clubs' events around the city. This group of women from Eastern Europe were all in Riyadh independently, working in hospitals. The hospitals housed them in shared accommodation and they did not have access to their own transport. They were an inspiring group – intelligent, assertive and energetic. One woman in particular – Martina – was a formidable asset as a club committee member, with her ruthless efficiency and direct attitude. Over time, I fell into a kind of friendship with Peter, based on him provoking me by being even more sexist than usual and me squaring up to him at every chauvinistic remark. I would tell my daughters that his views belonged in a museum – in front of him. In return, he told them that their mother should be at home baking cakes for them instead of going off to run races. Like Conrad, he had been in Riyadh for decades on his own, supporting a family back in UK, with expensive tastes in hobbies and holidays.

Spending time with men like Peter made David and me reflect on our fathers, both of whom had spent large parts of our childhood away from the family, working as expats in Asia. Of course, everyone's family circumstance is different but, with discomfort, I realised that for some people being away from one's family, particularly the demands of children, was easier than I would have liked to think. For some, living and working as a long-term expat, sending home generous and regular wads of money, whilst simultaneously enjoying one's job, hobbies and friends, without having to fit in with the rhythms or daily demands of other family members, was the preferable option. Your career could flourish, you could hone your athletic fitness or golf swing and your family could live in top-of-the-range comfort back at home. Instead of the drip-drip of routine days with your family, you could have short bursts of "quality time" on exciting or luxurious holidays together: on safari in Kenya or on a hired yacht in the Caribbean.

Perhaps the sceptre of loneliness in compound-life appeared bleak, but on our compound, almost a third of residents were expat men whose families were back in their homeland. As long as you didn't have the charisma of a cockroach or dubious personal hygiene, an active social life was definitely on the cards. To prove this point: when the compound mothers and children returned in September, after two months' school summer holidays usually spent in their homelands – some of the fathers showed signs of considerable wear and tear after those months of the single life on the compound. I heard tales of all-night poker sessions, fuelled by homemade grog, and regular beer and curry get-togethers. Definitely a case of the old adage: "When the cat's away, the mice will play." I liked to visualise the scenes in some villas when the calendar page was turned to September. Maids are exhorted to do a deep clean everywhere; fridges restocked to house more than just home-brewed beer and a jar of salsa dip; fruit bowls which had collected poker change, now proudly showcased the "five a day" requirement for the children. If there was also a freshly baked cake sitting on the kitchen counter for my return, the alarm bells would have been deafening.

I also saw the other side of the riyal: a friend would regularly struggle with the "mean reds" – as endured by Holly Golightly in 'Breakfast at Tiffany's' – after calling his family back in Germany, only to find that no one had the time to talk to him. When he managed to pin someone down to the phone, his three teenage children generally did not update him much on their lives, or show any interest in his – although they were quick to put in requests for extra money for a school ski trip or an upgrade to their current techno gadget. My friend seemed to fulfil the role of a distant, mythical money-tree.

This lifestyle was brought even closer to home for me when I decided in September 2010 that I would remain in Riyadh for no more than one more school year, returning to UK the following summer. David was supportive of my reasons for wanting to return to UK, but it was not something he wanted. He loved most aspects of his life in Riyadh. Because of our genders, we had starkly divergent experiences of life there. He enjoyed his job hugely – the challenge of the new project he was involved in; the independent way he was able to get on with his work; the almost fortnightly travelling. In fact, he said that the only downside of the travelling was my complaints about him being away from home so often. He also relished the lifestyle outside work – the weather, all the athletics he did with the Wheelers and Tri Club, weekend afternoons with his children at the pool made even more salubrious with the poolside bar open. Whilst I had an urgent need to get off the compound at weekends, he was happy to stay on it, as he had often spent part of the week away, out of Riyadh. And loathe as I am to admit it, I was tapped on the shoulder by the realisation that my formerly feminist-leaning partner had come to enjoy all the monotonous domestic tasks totally taken over by me in Riyadh – the grocery shopping, laundry, covering all the children's school holidays or sick days off school. Without a doubt, life was much harder for him in UK, when we both worked, and he had to juggle and share these tasks with me.

I offered him a deal: I would return with Riya and Shivani in July 2011, giving him the chance to stay on for a year on his own. Dramatically, I declared: "If you let me go, I will consider returning in two years' time." How this developed forms another chapter of my Riyadh story.

Occasionally, I had some contact with interesting, talented people, which lifted me out of my rut for a while. I met Lindsay on the compound bus, on one of my rare forays to a coffee morning. It was the school holidays and an American compound was hosting an American Independence Day event – something different to do off compound with the children. Lindsay kept anxiously checking her mobile. She explained that she was expecting a text at any moment, summoning her to Italy. In answer to my questions: no, she wasn't Italian, and no, she didn't have an ill family member there. Lindsay was a private Italian tutor in a branch of the Saudi royal family. She was a qualified Italian teacher from USA and had been in post in Riyadh for two years.

Supposedly, Italy is a popular holiday destination for rich Saudis. If they don't already own a home there, then they will often hire a house to escape to during the hot summer months in Riyadh. Schools in Riyadh – both private international and state-run ones – shut for around two months over the hottest months of the year – July and August. Expat mothers tended to escape with their children for an extended stay in their homeland. Expat fathers took as much leave as they were able to, to spend some time with their families out of Riyadh. David took a week's leave at the beginning and end of our summer holiday, to join us back in UK. This was typical for most expat fathers. From anecdotes, I gathered that the situation was often very different for Saudi working fathers. They appeared to be able to absent themselves from their jobs for the entire summer – to remain in supervision of their holidaying wives and children. As I grimly prepared myself for two months of solo daily childcare, it was hard to not be irrationally jealous of the "supervision" I was missing out on.

Lindsay's employer owned a villa in Italy. Thus, having a private Italian tutor was a useful appendage to this family, alongside the private English tutor, music teachers and personal trainers that many very rich Saudi families retain. Riya's PE school teacher also worked as a personal trainer to a prince, so PE lessons often abruptly ceased when his main employer decided to spend a month in Bahrain, or some other salubrious location. Mr Philip, the PE teacher, had to drop everything to accompany the prince, ready to do training with him whenever it fitted into his schedule.

Lindsay explained that she had travelled straight to Italy with her employer's family last summer, to act as a translator in addition to providing Italian tuition for the children during the summer. This year, the family were travelling through other European countries first before reaching Italy. This trip had involved a frenzy of organisation, as the family was large and the necessary retinue of staff, such as nannies, tutors, personal trainer and so on, added considerably to the numbers. Amidst this hubbub, they had "forgotten" to add Lindsay to the list. She had been luxuriating in some unexpected time off but was now on high alert for her summons, as the family had reached Italy. In a matter of hours, they would be searching amongst their entourage for their Italian translator and her absence would be discovered. My brain boggled at this type of lifestyle and I was desperate to "dig for some dirt" regarding what her job was really like. However, Lindsay was very discreet and, no doubt, very mindful of the venerable position she was in. She had a more than decent employment package, including the rent of her villa on an expat compound and a driver available to take her to and from her employer's palace. Although there were times when she was called to work at short notice, or had to work late into the night, to fit in with Saudi hours, at least she was able to have a separate life outside work. Those in posts such as a personal trainer may be required to live in the family's home, to be available at any hour of the day. Lindsay's work involved a fair amount of travelling, within Saudi Arabia, the Middle East and Europe. As a young, single woman, she savoured all the good things that this job gave her, for at least the short-term future. I admired her attitude but wished she would have been just a little less discreet.

I got to know another woman working in Riyadh as a private English tutor in a different Saudi royal household. She was a Professor in English Literature and Drama from the USA. Her work as a tutor usually started in the afternoon, when her charges returned from school. Sometimes she was required to actually attend their school lessons with them, if there was a particular subject they were struggling with. Usually, her mornings were free though. I was concerned that spending so much time in the company of children was causing the slow drip-drip away of the former sharpness of my mind, my coherence and my ability to discuss and debate with adults. I knew I was capable of more than sharing ideas on the contents of healthy packed lunch boxes – but for how much longer? Katherine seemed to share my concerns, even though she was paid well for her hours with young children, in contrast to me, who was, of course, paid double in terms of boundless love and eternal gratitude. To this end, Katherine set up a Shakespeare study group. This was not at all like some of the compound Book Clubs I had heard about; our fortnightly study group sessions felt far more like being back at university. We had to read the text before we met and consider it in the light of themes provided by Katherine. Katherine then gave us an in-depth tutorial on it, before we discussed issues, episodes and characters.

These classes always provided a stimulating break from yet another solitary morning studying for my law course. I made a wry observation that the membership of the study group comprised a very small number of women, whose attendance was not always regular. Turn-out at coffee mornings was invariably high – whether it was a large, compound-run event or a private get-together at someone's villa. This dichotomy spoke volumes about the preferred habits of many female compound residents – an issue Katherine and I shared many an eye-rolling grimace over.

I could count on the fingers of one hand the few people who became close friends during my life in Riyadh. The people I most enjoyed spending time with were, typically, those with the least spare time as they had jobs. Of course, this was exactly why I sought out their company; there was such a variety of subjects to talk about with them, and they had rich experiences of Riyadh life beyond the compound walls. One of my friends was a fellow running and triathlon club member. She also cycled with Riyadh Wheelers. Somehow she fitted all this activity in around her job as a full-time nurse in a hospital. She had an adventurous spirit and had come to Riyadh to work as a nurse in her early twenties, with a couple of other nursing friends from her home in Scotland. The infrequent interaction I had with her group of friends told me that they were assertive, fun-loving and down-to-earth women, who balanced the many frustrations and difficulties of working in Riyadh by grabbing all the positive opportunities available – going to Dubai to watch the rugby sevens tournament; splurging some of their salaries on designer handbags and shoes; and saving money to redeem a mortgage on a property back in UK. Moreover, single, eligible young women expats were still somewhat of a novelty, far outnumbered by men in the same bracket – so romance and a love life were definite features in their lives. It was hard to not be dazzled by their experiences, energy and social life.

After a particularly painful few months at the beginning of 2010, David became worried about the possibility of me fleeing Riyadh with the children earlier than planned. He decided to send me away for my own good and booked a night at Luthan Spa, a boutique, women-only hotel in Riyadh, where some months later I was called for an interview as a yoga teacher. It was an intriguing experience, which gave me a luxurious 24-hour break from family duties. It also confirmed to me that I was very much at odds with the modern Saudi way of life.

The hotel was beautiful and immaculate. As this was "women-only territory", women were allowed to work here. The beauty therapists and masseuses all appeared to be Filipino; the exercise class instructors represented a range of nationalities; and the receptionists were mainly Indian. After dropping off my bags, I wandered around the hotel. I felt like a crash investigator on the Marie Celèste: there was no one to be seen. The receptionist told me that the hotel's 25 rooms were almost all booked. By the end of my one night's stay, I was convinced that she had spun me a yarn for marketing purposes. I was the lone hotel guest at every activity I did – from using the various steam rooms and saunas to recovering post-massage with a cup of green tea in the lounge, and even when piling my plate up at the breakfast buffet. The exercise class I went along to had three other participants, but they were all members of Luthan's gym, not hotel guests.

I had a calm solo dinner with my book in the hotel's restaurant, trying not to think about how much a glass of wine would complete my day. Considering I was the only diner, the restaurant staff seemed surprisingly busy, taking telephone calls and bustling off with trays of food. I got into conversation with a waitress who told me that their Saudi guests tended to order room service, rather than coming to the restaurant. The rooms were splendid, but I chose to eat my dinner at a table in the restaurant, with views across the city, rather than on a tray on my bed, in a hotel room, in front of the wide-screen TV. It felt sad to me that a group of people who are so often kept indoors, with little freedom of movement, continue to shut themselves away from general public mingling even in the safe environment of a women-only hotel. On the other hand, it struck me as I turned my lights out at the decadent hour of 10 – a good hour past my usual, school-night bedtime – that I was probably missing the busiest period at the hotel.

As I have described earlier, the Saudi way of life favours the hours of darkness rather than those during the sun's worst glare and 40-degree heat. Fortified by their dinners, the day's prayer times now behind them, my fellow hotel guests were most likely crowding the pool, saunas and lounge areas, with no intention of retiring before the early hours of the morning. Refreshed after a 7am lie-in, I went to swim some lengths before breakfast, feeling spoilt by having the fairy tale facilities to myself, but also so lonely after spending almost 24 hours with little human contact – as alone as a typical week-day morning spent in front of my computer screen. The deep need to be amongst my close friends and like-minded people again threatened to make me drop like a stone to the pool's bottom. A timely moment for a latte and pastries.

Repatriation

On a typical British June day – weather neither indicative of summer nor spring – we landed at Heathrow, Saudi expats no longer. For the past two school summer holidays, I had returned to UK for two months with my daughters. Thus I was familiar with that surreal feeling of having journeyed from another world: where women were shrouded in black; SUVs transporting bearded men in white thobes charged erratically around the highways; and tanned expats emerged from the security gates of walled compounds. This arrival was different. I was shocked to find how sad I suddenly felt for the ending of that era. Shivani and Riya were full of vigour despite the missed night's sleep and spilt the beans on all our intimate details to other passengers on the shuttle bus to the car hire site. I looked out of the window, filled to the brim with emotion to hear them report that, "We live in Bristol now. We used to live in Riyadh." Children have no idea how lucky they are to be able to pick up and dispense with identities and labels so easily. In contrast, I continued informing inquisitive people that "I've recently returned from living in Riyadh" for a nonsensical length of time.

The last few weeks of our Saudi life had been unsurprisingly busy: selling unwanted items; selecting what things to ship; and organising "masalamas" (farewell parties). We also had to reserve a special pot of energy and enthusiasm to celebrate our daughters' birthdays. I was hugely relieved and grateful when Shivani asked to just have one of her closest friends over for a sleep-over for her birthday treat. Riya, in turn, was thrilled to have a whole party dedicated to her for the first time in Riyadh, rather than having to share the occasion with Shivani, as had happened for the past two years. Their birthdays are a week apart. David and I decidedly did not have the will to organise separate parties two weeks in a row, particularly as the June heat of Riyadh made anything other than a pool party pretty impossible. Hence Riya and Shivani had shared a party since we moved to Saudi.

I cannot miss this opportunity to describe what expat children's birthday parties could be like in Riyadh. While David and I stuck to our cheap 'n' cheerful formula of pool parties, Shivani and Riya had the privilege of being invited to parties featuring professional face-painters, bouncy castles, clowns and pony rides. Some expat children's parties ran on "AMT" (Arabic maybe time): the invitation said 3-7pm, but only my daughters and I would be there for the first hour, at which point the other guests would start trickling in. Similarly, I would have booked our taxi to collect us before 7pm: to beat what I had assumed would be a stampede out of the door at 7. This inevitably made us the earliest to leave. I found departure from certain parties very embarrassing, as my daughters were bestowed with "party bag" gifts that were bigger and more expensive than the birthday gift I had brought along for the event's boy or girl. I continued giving the kind of gifts that had been popular at the UK children's parties I had memories of: packs of mini stretchy snakes, pots of alien goo, wind-up tarantulas. The party bags Riya and Shivani got in return for our humble offerings included a space hopper, a lunchbox, dolls and, at the memorable pony ride party, Riya was offered a bulging bag of water – home to a goldfish – which I claimed we would not be allowed to take in the taxi. I once saw a group of Saudi children leaving a birthday party held at a local mall's play-zone, clutching plastic tubs, in which a fluffy coloured chick tumbled about in – a party bag extraordinaire. Shivani and Riya were as mortified as I was at the spectacle. Concerned that Riyadh might be running low on pastel-coloured chicks, David and I stuck to our own style of party bags. One year, we gave every departing child a pot plant, asking them to bring it back to next year's birthday party, so we could see how much it had grown. The next year, the girls' adopted uncle on the compound got his hands on a box of miniature torches through his work, which all the children got in a frenzy over. For Riya's last party, held a few weeks before we exited Riyadh, I emptied out my fiercely-guarded present box. "Close your eyes!" I would sternly order my daughters whenever I got the box out to select a present to be taken to a child's birthday party. That day, the children got a lucky dip choice including little bags of stretchy plastic snakes, life-size squidgy eyeballs and packs of plasticine.

We invariably left parties with boxes of left-over food, as some expats seemed to need to prove their wealth by going completely over-the-top in the range and amount of food available. Shivani went to a school friend's disco party, where each corner of the room featured a different world cuisine: noodles and stir fry; pizza and pasta; hamburgers and hotdogs; hummus and olives. I was brought up with a horror of wasting food – there's no amount of left-overs too small for me to save and incorporate into another meal. Hence, if the party's hostess urged me to take food home for "my hubbie", I never needed to be asked twice. Then the girls and I would stagger out to our awaiting taxi, with take-away boxes stacked up in my arms, a balloon tied to each girl's wrist and their own arms fiercely wrapped around the party bag gift – just in case the birthday boy or girl decided that our paltry offering did not merit recompense, after all.

My admiration of my daughters was perhaps at its zenith at the first birthday party they were invited to on our return to UK. A mere few weeks in their dusty past, they had gone to a lovely party in a gleaming, new mall in Riyadh, boasting a climbing wall, table football and fancy dress room. Pan the camera back to the party in Bristol, which we were invited to by a mother of a girl from Riya's class. We arrived punctually as ever – an intractable habit not ground down by the Saudi years – unfazed to be the first arrivals. However, our calm demeanour was tested a little to discover that the mother had not even begun decorating the community centre hall where the party was being held. She also smelt quite strongly of alcohol – quite understandably, it was a day for her to celebrate too. My wonderful, adaptable daughters took it all in their stride and began blowing up balloons. I rearranged my face into a less judgemental expression and busied myself with making cheese and pineapple on sticks, getting out the paper plates and filling bowls with crisps. By the time the birthday girl arrived with her Dad, the hall looked a tad more festive. Laying down my cheese-cutting knife, I looked at my daughters tearing around, half blowing up balloons before letting them off round the room, collapsing with giggles at the loud raspberry noises emitted – and marvelled at their magnificence. No pony rides, no party bags, no games organised – but they seemed delighted with a bag of balloons and the fact that they had got direct access to all the party food before anyone else had arrived. On the way home, I casually mentioned that this party had been a bit different from those in Riyadh. Their response involved a mere shrug of the shoulders and "I suppose so".

Back to our departure from Riyadh: I decided not to have an advertised American-style yard sale, *de rigueur* for departing residents, because there were so many on the compound at that time. As usual, the impending school summer holidays brought with it the permanent departure of a generous sprinkling of residents. Expats either relocating to new posts or returning home, who had children, tried to time their moves during the summer school holidays, so their children would be able to start their new school at the beginning of the academic year. In my boot-camp sergeant mode, I planned for my daughters to join their new school in UK for the last three weeks of the summer term. On a practical level, this gave me time to get our home up-and-running, whilst childcare and education were thoughtfully provided by their school, rather than me. It also had a huge attraction for me as it cut down the dreaded two-and-a-half-month school summer holidays I had gritted my teeth through for two previous years. On a compassionate, child-centred level, it also proved a huge benefit to Shivani and Riya settling happily back to school in September; all the initial nervousness about starting their new school had been tackled during those three weeks in July.

Instead of the flood of a yard sale, I sold things on a trickle basis. I would tell Flora, my wonderful babysitter, and Nina, who cleaned our villa once a week, the latest items I had de-weeded and their price. They either bought them themselves, or spread the word amongst the highly efficient social networking channels that existed, from mobile to mobile, between all the domestic workers and drivers on the compound. In the weeks leading up to our departure, I did begin to feel increasingly hounded by unfamiliar maids and drivers, who made a beeline for me when I was out and about on the compound, to badger me to let them know first about what I was selling that week. Their mobile phone numbers on scraps of paper were thrust at me, to ensure their direct access to my sales hotline. It didn't seem to matter how many sales were held on the compound, selling the familiar items of kettle, pillows and ironing board, the domestic workers and drivers always thronged to villas at the merest hint of a sale. Getting in conversation with some friends of Flora's who came to view some of my sale items in their lunch break, I learnt why these sales were not only popular but vital to them. The majority of their purchases were sent back home to their families – to the Philippines, Sri Lanka, Bangladesh. Toys winged their way to children being brought up by grandparents; fans cooled rooms in houses paid for by remittances from Riyadh; Tupperware boxes held left-over Pinoy hot and sour soup, Sri Lankan uppama and Bangladeshi channa dahl. Yard sales were the equivalent of eBay, charity shops, car boot sales and Trade-It, all rolled into one. Here, the wages of the drivers and domestic workers could be stretched out over an extended amount of purchases.

With two days to go to D-Day – departure day – our shipping boxes began their long journey from Riyadh to Bristol. The exit out of Riyadh customs in itself had the potential of being a saga. The morning with the packers had been partly relaxing and partly a phenomenon, at which I was an innocent bystander. David and I had made piles of shipping items on table tops, kitchen corners, in the middle of rooms. The five packers worked soundlessly, efficiently and at a terrific speed, making all the piles vanish. Ditto for the plates of biscuits and jugs of juice I left out for them on a regular basis. David and I found a useful link with them: they were all Filipino men, as were many of the members of Riyadh Wheelers. David rattled off some names of Filipino cyclists who were really good, or who he had got on with particularly well – and the packers knew all of them.

Whenever we managed to persuade them to stop for a 10-minute tea break, we all sat around, chatting about the Wheelers, cycling, running and triathlons. I felt so lucky that one of our last days on our compound had such a lovely glow and connectivity encapsulated in it. It seemed slightly illicit that a process that should be so stressful – packing up your home to relocate to a different country – actually required no physical effort on my part and entailed such enjoyable social interaction with total strangers.

Buoyed by this feel-good atmosphere, David and I advertised the very last drip of unwanted items. The banks broke open and our villa surged with most of the compound's domestic workers and drivers. Flora and I sat in giggling disbelief on the sofa, swayed by the fact that we would have to say goodbye to each other in a few hours' time, as David extravagantly kept selling items for 50 halala. There are 100 halala in a riyal and at that time, there were six riyals to the pound. In other words, David sold most items that day for 10p. He even sold the flip flops he was standing in at the time, so carried away was he with the showmanship of the moment. I learnt that day that lurking somewhere in my partner was a Del Boy Trotter, searching for an appropriate street corner to flog his goods on.

I allowed the whirlwind of all this to distract me from what I was leaving behind. More importantly, I was very focused on the horizon – on the UK life I was going to return to. Inevitably, it takes the absence of something to make you realise its value. The "cabin fever" I often experienced from compound-life and the distance I tried to maintain from the "coffee-morning culture" seemed slightly regrettable to me once I was away from it all. The openness, generosity and quick warmth of the expat community only really struck me when I returned to my home in UK. Here, I had to put in all the leg-work to help my daughters and myself reintegrate into UK life. I found that I had to make all the effort to re-kindle my former friendships, or to try to get my older daughter involved again with her previous circle of friends. It is obvious why it had to be like this: we were the ones who went away, whilst everyone else continued their lives in UK without us. Friends who were red-eyed at my departure, claiming that they "didn't know what they'd do without me", picked themselves up, got back on the horse and did very well indeed without me. Of course it had to fall to me to remind them, repeatedly, that they did not have to continue doing without me or my family any more. Whilst I generally felt no rancour for this, it did make me reflect on how different it was to be a newcomer on the compound in Riyadh. As there were relatively few families with young children when my daughters and I first moved there, we were sought out almost immediately by other parents and children. Those first knocks on the door for "Shivani and Riya to come out and play" did not take long to be heard. Parents immediately told me about what activities were available on the compound for children and where Shivani had to wait for the school bus. Once it was known that Riya would be going to the school on the compound, rather than the British school like Shivani, one thoughtful mother promptly offered to look after Shivani on the school bus, to help me with the practicalities of getting two children to two different schools at the same time – something that I had not even begun to think through yet. I became immensely grateful for her daily kindness in covering Shivani's "school run".

Other expat adults, in the meanwhile, showed genuine interest in our back-story. Was this our first expat posting? Where had we moved from? Did we need anything before our shipping arrived? As everyone had been through the relocation process at least once, there was a common understanding that new residents may be without their worldly goods for a few weeks, awaiting their shipping. I remember the frustration of one family who knew their shipping had arrived in the country but was held up in Customs for almost a month: so near, yet so far. Riya and I used to do a weekly drop-off of toys and books for the family's children until their boxes finally arrived. Riya then brazenly used the leverage of our previous toy-loan service to ask to borrow some of Zadie's toys in return, the little girl in the family. Moving back to our UK neighbourhood was a contrast to this. Most people in our locality seemed pleased and surprised to see us back – "Gosh. That went quickly!" However, any practical help was slow in coming: no loan offers of the odd saucepan or mug. Our neighbours' general experience of moving was not on an international scale, so belongings usually arrived at the same time as the people, with none of the time-lag we had between our arrival and that of our precious boxes. By pure coincidence, serving to emphasise the point, one of our neighbours moved to a nearby area, a few weeks after our return. Everything was shifted during school hours, so their children were picked up from school and taken to their new home, with all their creature comforts intact around them immediately. Shivani and Riya, in the meanwhile, had to make do with the few toys and games I had packed in our suitcases for many weeks. We used to do weekly trips to the local library, luxuriating in using a library we didn't have to run ourselves. We then staggered home, rucksacks laden with 20 or so books – to fill our otherwise empty bookshelves.

Aside from the lack of practical help, we found questions about our Saudi experience were superficial for the main part; the questioner visibly glazed over if I went into too much detail, a notorious fault of mine even at the most rushed of times. By Day Two of our repatriation, David and I exchanged amused looks as we overheard each other using the same standard stock-phrase: "It was an adventure." We had learnt that this vivid, multi-faceted answer served the greatest good for the greatest number. We resolved to be Saudi bores in private, in our home only. Again, it is totally understandable why most people who had continued day-to-day life in UK didn't want to hear about driving to Bahrain for the weekend; BBQs in the desert on Boxing Day; or that Riya had been taught French and Arabic at her school since the age of three. Tales of less attractive aspects of Saudi life had slightly more appeal – such as being reprimanded by the muttawa in the supermarket – but even then, the briefer, the better. I am not completely self-absorbed all the time, so I was interested to hear about the lives of people in my neighbourhood on my return. I had kept in contact with very close friends and family during the Riyadh years, via regular emails and visits when I was back in UK in the summers with my daughters. Perhaps unsurprisingly, the quality of update I got from those who were acquaintances rather than friends was pretty mediocre. Following one awkward silence with a neighbour, who was clearly not interested in receiving more than a three-word answer in response to her question about how the past two years had been for me, I was relieved to be informed that her cat was still alive. I also was left floundering for an appropriate reaction when the lovely man from up the road, upon seeing me for the first time in over two years, immediately shared his disappointment over his allotment produce compared to last year's crop.

Both our parents had warned me and David to not feel deflated when we returned. They shared their own experiences of similar conversations with neighbours that had left them feeling as if they had never been away at all. For me, there was a comfort to it, despite the gloominess it also evoked in me. I had been spoilt, surrounded by high-earning expats who described previous postings in Tokyo and LA; renovation projects for their rustic Spanish villa; and training plans for the next Ironman in Hawaii. Although, thankfully, for us dedicated "family PAs", conversations about healthy lunchbox snacks and where to get the cheapest school shoes are to be found whether in Riyadh or Bristol.

This of course does not give the full picture. There were people, not even necessarily particularly close friends or family, who themselves had travelled or had a larger world view, who were enthusiastically interested in learning about our lives in Riyadh. There were also people who were a fantastic support to me, who reminded me what a difficult thing it had been for an ambitious woman with illusions of independence to do; and what an achievement it was for the four of us. Those conversations left a rosy glow. As both David's and my parents had been expats for so long – and David's twin brother and family were expats in India while we were in Riyadh – there tended to be an accepting, matter-of-fact attitude about our own expat episode within our families. In fact, when we returned to UK, it was not long before one of our family members asked the question: "So, where next?" In Riyadh itself, we had been surrounded by others doing the same thing, many of whom were career expats, moving all over the globe, from post to post – so there was no back-patting from that quarter, either. What we did remains out of the ordinary and I am so grateful to those people who helped keep that fresh for me.

I wryly describe my Riyadh years as the "gift that keeps giving". I returned with fire in my belly to be economically active again, to get back to my former financial fighting weight and put to use my law qualification that I had committed an anti-social life to. There was a further ulterior motive: I desperately needed to extend my day-to-day life experiences beyond the walls of my home and compound. My obsessive compulsive disorder regarding the minutiae of domestic life, which had crept up on me in Riyadh, now threatened to engulf me. I had allowed my focus to become narrower and narrower, as my daily tasks honed in on packing PE kits, cooking all the meals, doing all the laundry – because I felt so keenly the lack of financially contributing to the family. I scanned the pages of my diaries from those Riyadh years and was appalled to see how many of my goals and actions were about running the business of family, with no reference to the training courses, management committee meetings or staff supervision appointments that had formerly also peppered my diary. I wanted to remember who I used to be.

Staggering under the heavy weight of all these expectations on my shoulders, I returned to UK after almost three years' absence. The cherry on top was the intimidating state of the UK job market I returned to. I feel proud of myself that, despite the reality, I managed to keep energetic and optimistic for so long in the face of job rejection after job rejection. Even getting interviews seemed a Herculean achievement. My former work experience in the voluntary and community sector was now three years out of date, and I was competing in a market flooded with people with similar but fresher skills, as many of these organisations had shut down due to the new "austerity" funding issues. Trying to take my Paralegal qualification into the legal world was as insurmountable, as I had absolutely no experience in that sector.

Leaving Riyadh, I had been giddy at the thought of the amount of child-free school hours I could offer a prospective employer, not realising that there were far more people seeking jobs who were available full-time, for flexible hours; not to mention the salient fact that job-seekers outnumbered vacancies in recession Britain. After hearing my woes about not even being called in for interviews with recruitment consultants at agencies, three close friends – all assertive, successful minority ethnic women – gave their take on the situation, gently but with their usual brutal honesty: "You are academically over-qualified for the posts you are applying for. You have not been employed since July 2008. You can only offer part-time hours. You are a minority ethnic woman. Any or all of these factors plays a part in employers not being interested in you." After my experiences of racism in Saudi Arabia, I refused to believe that this same mythological Hydra would rear one of its many heads in my life back in UK. Living with the lack of freedom and equality in Riyadh, I had idolised UK life, with its human rights and equalities legislation, its freedom of expression and tolerance and its opportunities. In doing so, I deliberately chose to forget past personal experiences of prejudice there.

I decided it was time for a mini sociology experiment: to either rebut or prove the truth of my friends' words. I registered on-line with yet another recruitment agency, this time using a more Western sounding first name and David's surname. I attached a CV that had also been a little doctored, using my pseudonym and David's email address. Whereas almost every other recruitment agency I had registered with on-line had sent me an email 24 hours later – "Thanks but no thanks" – this recruitment agency replied back within the hour, asking me to go in and have a face-to-face registration interview. My emotions were so mixed. It was hardly an outcome I could feel victorious about; I felt more disappointed than angry. After some further advice and counselling from one of the trio who had helped instigate this situation, I went to the interview and ended the charade by giving my actual name and explaining why I had applied under a pseudonym. Naturally, the recruitment consultant was wide-eyed with horror at the thought that other agencies may have chosen not to see me on the grounds of my name and ethnicity. She claimed the moral upper-hand by declaring that she would have wanted to interview me regardless of which name I had used. Sadly, after this warming, bonding experience, I never heard from her again. Doubtless, she felt unable to market me to prospective employers in the knowledge of what a conniving, duplicitous character I was.

My little experiment did me no favours. After that, I found myself in a predicament every time I put in a job application, wondering which name to use. I am fiercely proud of both my name and cultural heritage but now felt paranoid every time I got a job rejection – and I had to keep fielding those punches – that these were the responsible factors in my continuing unemployed status. On my spiral downwards, another thought occurred to me. My CV and job applications obviously cited that I had spent the last two-plus years living in Saudi Arabia, working as a yoga teacher. As a dear friend pointed out, if I made no reference to those years and left them as a blank, people might think I'd been in prison for all that time. I wondered whether prospective employers would know that my name was not a Muslim or Middle Eastern one. I had an epiphany: perhaps they thought I had spent the last two years at a madrasa in Saudi Arabia, educating myself in a more fundamentalist Islam than had been available to me in UK. Teaching yoga had merely been a front for my religious studies. When I shared my misgivings with David, he equally despaired of the state of my mind that led me to such "discoveries" but could not dismiss the idea completely. Trialling a sociological experiment in this particular theory proved even beyond my conniving and duplicitous nature.

Almost five months after my "repatriation", I allowed myself to contemplate the irony that I had earned more on the compound through teaching yoga than I seemed able to do in UK, where I could not even market myself as a yoga teacher as I wasn't formally qualified. Maybe the remains of my "runaway" fund – the hoarded yoga class riyals – could be stretched for a ticket back to Riyadh, one way only…

Now is the time for this masalama. I occasionally touch base with myself, questioning whether I have regrets – either about going to Riyadh in the first place, or about returning. In Sufism – an ancient and more mystical form of Islam – there is a belief that dwelling in the past or the future veils a person from life itself. Although I personally don't find it easy to live by this principle, I believe it is right. I overheard my daughters the other day, trying to remember the name of a child they had once played with in a swimming pool somewhere. They went through the different pools that they've swum in, in various locations around the world, trying to resolve the quandary: on our compound? In Bahrain? At Bentota? With no shame at all, I admit that my children are spoilt – not with possessions but with the rich diversity of experiences their short lives have already encompassed. The culture and expat way of life in Riyadh encouraged us to seize what opportunities we could. We are continuing to live like that back home. It was an adventure; no more need be said.